Vocabulary Explorations

Level C

Lesli J. Favor, Ph.D.

Steven L. Stern

Amsco School Publications, Inc.
315 Hudson Street New York, N.Y. 10013

About the Authors

Lesli J. Favor

Lesli J. Favor holds a Ph.D. in English from the University of North Texas. After graduating, she was assistant professor of English at Sul Ross State University Rio Grande College, in southwest Texas. She left that position to write full-time for publishers of books for school classrooms and libraries. She is the author of twenty English/language arts and nonfiction texts, in addition to coauthoring this three-volume vocabulary series. She lives near Seattle with her husband, young son, two dogs, and horse.

Steven L. Stern

Steven L. Stern has more than 30 years of experience as a writer and textbook editor, developing a wide range of books, educational products, and informational materials for children and adults. He has written many test-preparation books and is the author of two novels as well as numerous articles and short stories. He has also worked as an English teacher, a lexicographer, and a writing consultant. Mr. Stern lives in New Jersey.

Reviewers:

Jessica Bennett, Language Arts Teacher, Brookpark Middle School, and Membership Co-Chair, Ohio Council of Teachers of English Language Arts, Columbus, Ohio

Elizabeth Henley, Language Arts Teacher, Ardsley Middle School, Ardsley, New York

Julia Shepherd, Language Arts and History Teacher, Arizona Middle School, Riverside, California

Cover Design: Nesbitt Graphics, Inc.
Text Design and Composition: Nesbitt Graphics, Inc.
Cartoons: Angela Martini

Please visit our Web site at: *www.amscopub.com*

When ordering this book, please specify:
either **R 057 W** *or* VOCABULARY EXPLORATIONS, LEVEL C

ISBN: 978-1-56765-194-2
NYC Item 56765-194-1

Copyright © 2010 by Amsco School Publications, Inc.

No part of this book may be reproduced in any form without written permission from the publisher.

Printed in the United States of America

1 2 3 4 5 6 7 8 9 10   15 14 13 12 11 10 09

Contents

Understanding Shades of Meaning 207

Why and How to Use This Book

Why Vocabulary?

This book will help you expand your vocabulary and learn to think about words in different ways. But why is that important?

Having a strong vocabulary will help you communicate with people. Imagine that a friend asks you about your day. If you say that it was "fine," your friend will get a hint of what your day was like. But if you use a more specific word, like "routine," "tiring," or "fantastic," your friend will get a sharper picture of what you experienced. A larger vocabulary helps you communicate more clearly so that people can better understand your thoughts and ideas.

Using the right words also gives you power. If you want to write a successful job application or a convincing article or letter, choosing exact words will help your voice be heard.

The more words you know, the more you'll be able to read and understand in your daily life. You'll gain greater meaning from books, magazines, newspapers, and Web sites, and you'll develop a deeper understanding of issues in the world around you.

Increasing your vocabulary will improve your writing, reading, and speaking, in school and beyond. *Vocabulary Explorations* will help get you there.

About This Series

This is the third book of **Amsco's Vocabulary Program**, a complete line of vocabulary books for middle and high school students. In *Vocabulary Explorations*, **Levels A–C**, you'll awaken your knowledge of words. You'll study how words come into our language, how to figure out and understand meanings, and how to know which words to use. In *Vocabulary for the High School Student*, you'll sharpen your knowledge of word parts and increase your vocabulary. In *Vocabulary for the College-Bound Student*, you'll learn more challenging words that will help you tackle college-level readings and textbooks. Note that every book in The Amsco Vocabulary Program contains practice sections that will help you prepare for vocabulary questions on state tests and national tests like the PSAT, SAT, and ACT.

What's Inside This Book

Here in *Vocabulary Explorations, Level C* you will find a variety of lessons, features, and activities.

> **Sneak Peek: Preview the Lesson:** This quick activity will get you thinking about the topic of the mini-lesson.

> **Vocabulary Mini-Lessons:** These lessons introduce key vocabulary concepts and provide examples. The first lessons focus on word parts (prefixes, suffixes, roots) and building words. The next lessons explore the other ways words come into general use, crossing over from mythology, foreign languages, and technology into everyday speech and writing. In the last lessons, you'll focus on word meanings. How can you figure out the definitions of new words? What if a word has more than one meaning?

> **Words to Know: Lists and Activities:** In each chapter, you'll find two or more word lists. Each list contains five or ten vocabulary words and their meanings, as well as sample sentences. You're also given the pronunciation of each word (called the phonetic respelling because it helps you sound it out). After the word lists are three kinds of activities.

>> **Own It: Develop Your Word Understanding** helps you understand the meanings of the new words.

>> **Link It: Make Word-to-World Connections** has you make a personal connection to the words and learn how to use them in your own life.

>> **Master It: Use Words in Meaningful Ways** has you try using your new words in different ways.

> **Wrapping Up: Review What You've Learned.** This section summarizes what you've learned in the chapter.

> **Flaunt It: Show Your Word Understanding.** These exercises help you review the words in each chapter. The exercises will help you prepare for state and national tests.

> **Activities à la Carte: Extend Your Word Knowledge.** At the end of each chapter, you'll find these creative extension activities from which you or your teacher can choose. There's also an **ELL** option.

Oh, and one more thing. As you work through the book, you'll be greeted by **Word Master Mike**, who will use some of the vocabulary words to tell you about his own life. As he does so, you'll gain a better sense of how you, too, can use these words.

Hey, I'm Word Master Mike. I love learning new words and using them to talk about stuff in school and in my life. With a bigger vocabulary, I have more ways to express myself. As you work through this book, you'll get to know me better. I'll appear here and there to talk about my life, using new words from each chapter. See you later!

This book is an important resource that will increase your knowledge and understanding of words. Continue with the rest of The Amsco Vocabulary Program, and you'll see big improvements in your ability to speak and write effectively.

Good luck!
Lesli J. Favor, Ph.D. and Steven L. Stern, *Authors*
Lauren Davis, *Editor*

Learning Words Through Prefixes

Objectives

In this chapter, you will learn
> What a prefix is
> How and why to add prefixes
> Words with Greek, Latin, and Anglo-Saxon prefixes

Take a look at the messages printed on paper grocery bags. Chances are, you'll find one like this:

This bag is 100% recyclable and contains a minimum of 40% recycled material.

You may already recycle paper and plastic. The recycled material is used to make new products. Did you know that you can recycle words, too? Our language has *base words* (basic, complete words) and *roots* (main parts of words) that can be used over and over to create different words and meanings. How? By adding word parts such as a prefix. A **prefix** is added to the beginning of a base word or root to create a new word.

Think about the word *take*, for example. You can add the prefix *re-* to *take* to form *retake*. Then you can recycle *take* to form *mistake*. In this chapter, you'll learn a variety of prefixes and look at how they can be used to recycle base words and roots.

Sneak Peek: Preview the Lesson

Parts Department

The following organizer contains some of the prefixes, base words, and roots that you'll study in this lesson. How many words can you form using these parts? (You may use each part more than once.) Spend five minutes in the "parts department" putting words together. Then share your results with your classmates.

Prefixes		Base Words and Roots		
im-	anti-	dote	band	maneuver
fore-	contra-	mortal	biotic	most
ex-	poly-	gon	skilled	tract
semi-	out-	dict	last	sight

Words Formed from the Parts Above

Ⓥocabulary Mini-Lesson: All About Prefixes

The Parts of Words

Many words are made up of two or more parts. These parts may be prefixes or suffixes, base words or roots. You may already know these terms, but let's do a quick review.

> A **base word** is a complete word to which word parts may be added. For example, ***common**ly* and *un**common*** both contain the base word *common*.

> A **root** is a word part from which other words are formed. A root is different from a base word because a root usually cannot stand by itself. For example, ***vis**ion*, *in**vis**ible*, and ***vis**ual* all contain the Latin root *vis*, which means "see." You'll learn more about roots in Chapter 3.

> A **prefix** is a group of letters added to the beginning of a base word or root so as to create a new word. For example, adding the prefix *un-* to the base word *sure* creates the word ***un**sure*.

> A **suffix** is a group of letters added to the end of a base word or root so as to create a new word. For example, adding the suffix *-less* to the base word *fear* creates the word *fear**less***. You'll learn more about suffixes in Chapter 2.

Forming Words with Prefixes

In this chapter we'll focus on prefixes and how they form words. Like other word parts, every prefix has its own meaning. What new words are created when you add prefixes to the following base words?

PREFIX	+	BASE WORD	=	WORD
mis- (wrongly)	+	judge	=	*misjudge*

I try not to <u>misjudge</u> a person's character.

| *dis-*
(the opposite of) | + | connect | = | *disconnect* |

Please <u>disconnect</u> the lamp from the outlet.

Now imagine that instead of *mis-* and *dis-*, you added two different prefixes to those same base words.

PREFIX	+	BASE WORD	=	WORD
pre- (before)	+	judge	=	*prejudge*

Don't <u>prejudge</u> people on the basis of their appearance.

| *re-*
(again or back) | + | connect | = | *reconnect* |

Madison <u>reconnected</u> the computer after she repaired it.

By changing the prefix, you create new words.

Prefixes are added to roots just as they are to base words. Let's look at a couple of examples.

The root *cede* comes from Latin and means "to go." The root *ject* also comes from Latin and means "to throw." What words are formed by combining the following prefixes with these roots?

PREFIX	+	ROOT	=	WORD
pre-	+	*cede* (go)	=	*precede*

The letter *e* <u>precedes</u> *i* in the word *receive*.

| *re-* | + | *ject*
(throw) | = | *reject* |

The company <u>rejected</u> my application because it was incomplete.

Joining *pre-* with the root *cede* creates the word *precede*, which literally means "to go before." Joining *re-* with *ject* forms the word *reject*, which literally means "to throw back."

Why Learn This?

Knowing some common prefixes can help you figure out the meanings of unfamiliar words. When you learn a prefix, you have a key to unlocking the meaning of every word that begins with that prefix. For example, you may already know that the prefix *tri-* means three. This will give you a clue to the meaning of many words, such as

> *triangular*: shaped like a *triangle*, a figure with three angles and three sides
>
> *tripod*: a three-legged stand or support, as for a camera
>
> *triple*: three times as much or as many
>
> *trident*: a three-pronged spear

Knowing the meaning of *tri-* may not help you figure out *every* word with that prefix, but you'll always have a hint to get started. For example, imagine someone asks you to fill out a form in *triplicate*. Now that you know *tri-*, how many copies do you think there will be? If a new movie theater opens in your neighborhood, and it's a *triplex*, how many screens will it have?

Often you can figure out an unfamiliar word by combining your knowledge of the prefix with clues from the *context*, or surrounding words. Read the following sentence:

> Athletes came from the *tristate* area to compete in the *triathlon*.

Using your knowledge of *tri-* in combination with the context clues, can you figure out the meaning of the sentence? (Hint: *-athlon* comes from Greek and means "contest.")

A *triathlon* is an athletic contest consisting of three events. "*Tristate* area" refers to three neighboring states. You'll learn more about using context clues in Chapter 7.

Words to Know: Vocabulary Lists and Activities

Most prefixes in the English language come from Latin, Greek, or Anglo-Saxon (Old English). In this chapter, you will see examples of all three.

Here are a few things to keep in mind.

> ❯ A prefix may have just one meaning (*tri-* means "three"), or it may have more than one (*re-* means "again" or "back").

> ❯ Different prefixes can have the same meaning. For example, the Latin prefixes *non-* and *im-* and the Anglo-Saxon prefix *un-* all mean "not," as in *nonessential*, *immature*, and *unafraid*.

> Some prefixes are spelled in more than one way. For example, the prefix *com-* means "together," as in *compromise*. The prefix may also be spelled *con-*, as in *conspiracy*.

> Some words put two prefixes together. For example, *unpredictable* combines the two prefixes *un-* and *pre-* with the root *dict* ("tell or speak") and the suffix *-able*: *The weather is unpredictable.*

List 1   Words with Latin Prefixes

Study these four Latin prefixes and ten words that are formed with them. Read each word, what it means, and how it's used.

Prefix	Meaning	Examples
ad-	to or near	**ad**here, **ad**jacent, **ad**vocate
circum-	around	**circum**ference, **circum**navigate
contra-	against	**contra**band, **contra**dict
e-, ex-	out, from, or away	**e**ject, **e**lude, **ex**tract

Word	What It Means	How It's Used
adhere *(v)* ad-HEER	to stay attached; stick	This bumper sticker will not *adhere* to a wet surface.
adjacent *(adj)* uh-JAY-suhnt	next to; nearby	The ball field is *adjacent* to the school.
advocate *(v)* AD-vuh-kate	to plead in support of (literally, "to call to")	Both candidates *advocate* changes to our health-care system.
circumference *(n)* ser-KUHM-fer-ents	the line bounding a circle	The math teacher asked students to measure the *circumference* of the globe along the equator.
circumnavigate *(v)* sur-kuhm-NAH-vi-gate	to go completely around	Sir Francis Drake *circumnavigated* the world in the 16th century.
contraband *(n)* KON-truh-band	illegally imported or exported goods	Police arrested the smugglers and seized their *contraband*.

continued

contradict *(v)* kon-truh-DIKT	to state the opposite of; disagree with (literally, "to speak against")	Olivia's account of events *contradicts* Elliot's version.
eject *(v)* i-JEKT	to remove; throw out	The players were *ejected* from the game for fighting.
elude *(v)* i-LOOD	to avoid or escape	The criminal *eluded* capture for several days.
extract *(v)* ik-STRAKT	to draw out; pull out	The dentist had to *extract* my tooth.

Own It: Develop Your Word Understanding

Prefix Wheels

Directions: Work with a partner to complete the activity. For each prefix wheel, complete these steps:

1. Fill in the prefix wheel by writing the meaning of each word in the space provided.

2. Complete the sentences that follow the wheel. Use your knowledge of the key word to decide how to complete the sentence.

3. In the blank section of the wheel, write additional words that begin with the given prefix or prefixes.

Which does not **adhere** to paper: masking tape, glitter, or stickers? (circle one)

Who is sitting **adjacent** to you? _____

What change to the school lunch menu would you **advocate**?

_____

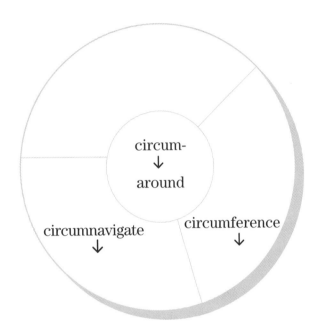

Which of your fingers has the smallest **circumference**?

_____

Which would you want to **circumnavigate**, a street fair or a traffic accident? (circle one)

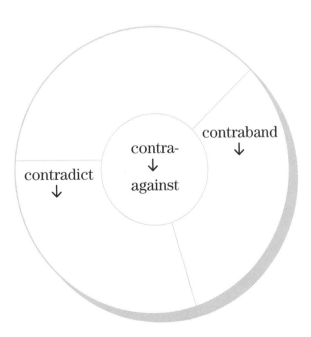

Name one item that would be **contraband** on school property.

_____

When have you **contradicted** something a friend said?

_____

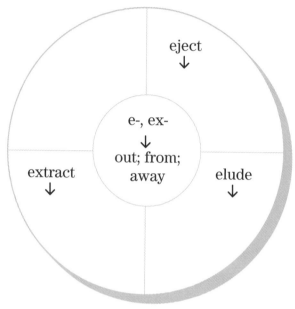

eject
↓

e-, ex-
↓
out; from;
away

extract
↓

elude
↓

How do you **eject** a DVD from a DVD player? _____

Name a reason why you might **elude** a friend. _____

_____

What could you use to **extract** a splinter from your finger? ____

_____

The front door to my house is <u>adjacent</u> to the kitchen. After school, I try to <u>elude</u> my mother so she doesn't ask me a million questions about my day. I slip in the side door instead, and <u>circumnavigate</u> the kitchen, where she has her afternoon coffee.

Link It: Make Word-to-World Connections

Have You Ever . . .

Directions: Most vocabulary words in the list are action verbs. How might you use one of these verbs—or the adjective or nouns in the list—to question classmates about their experiences? Follow these steps:

1. Use the words "Have you ever . . ." to form a question for your classmates. Examples are "Have you ever had peanut butter *adhere* to the roof of your mouth?" and "Have you ever played in a park *adjacent* to a lake?"

2. One by one, students ask their questions to the class. In response, people raise hands to indicate an answer of *yes*. Your teacher will call on people to explain their answers. (Example answer: "I had peanut butter *adhere* to the roof of my mouth. Then I discovered that mixing jam with the peanut butter keeps everything from *adhering*.")

Master It: Use Words in Meaningful Ways

Hot Topics

Directions: Link one of the vocabulary words to a current event or issue in your community. Here's what to do:

1. With the vocabulary words in mind, read, watch, or listen to local news. Be alert for ways to link a vocabulary word to topics in the news. For instance, you might link *adjacent* or *circumference* to news about construction projects. You might link *advocate*, *contraband*, or *elude* to coverage of crime or legal issues.

2. Write a one-minute news brief that you can read to your class. Be sure to use at least one vocabulary word in your news brief.

3. Your teacher will schedule students to read news briefs, a few per day, over the course of a week. As you listen to the news briefs, challenge yourself to identify each vocabulary word used. Your teacher may ask for an oral or written response regarding the words you identify.

List 2   Words with Latin Prefixes

Here are four additional Latin prefixes and ten useful words that contain them. Read each word, what it means, and how it's used.

Prefix	Meaning	Examples
im-, in-, ir-	not or the opposite of	**im**mortal, **in**competent, **ir**relevant
post-	after	**post**pone, **post**script, **post**war
semi-	partly	**semi**conscious, **semi**skilled
super-	above, over, or beyond	**super**ficial, **super**natural

Word	What It Means	How It's Used
immortal *(adj)* i-MAWR-tl	living forever; everlasting	The gods and goddesses of Greek mythology were *immortal*.
incompetent *(adj)* in-KOM-pi-tuhnt	not having enough ability or knowledge	The *incompetent* plumber flooded our kitchen.
irrelevant *(adj)* i-REH-luh-vuhnt	not related to the subject; beside the point	Tighten your essay by eliminating *irrelevant* details.
postpone *(v)* pohst-POHN	to put off until a later time; delay (literally, "to put after")	The storm forced us to *postpone* our meeting until tomorrow.
postscript *(n)* POHST-skript	a note added to a letter following the signature (literally, "to write after")	*Postscript* is abbreviated "P.S." at the end of a letter.
postwar *(adj)* POHST-WAWR	after a war	The *postwar* problems of Europe took years to overcome.
semiconscious *(adj)* seh-me-KON-shuhs	not fully conscious	The accident victim was *semiconscious* when the first-aid squad arrived.
semiskilled *(adj)* seh-me-SKILD	having limited skills or training	The company hired *semiskilled* laborers to move the furniture and load the trucks.
superficial *(adj)* soo-per-FIH-shuhl	limited to the surface; shallow	Fortunately, the car crash left the driver with only *superficial* injuries.
supernatural *(adj)* soo-per-NAH-chuh-ruhl	beyond what is usual or normal; that cannot be explained by the laws of nature	In many horror novels, *supernatural* forces control events.

> ## Tip
>
> Be alert for new words created by adding common prefixes to familiar base words. For example, the prefix *super-* is attached to many words these days, from *superhighway* and *supermodel* to *superstar* and *supersized.* What other "super" words can you think of?

Own It: Develop Your Word Understanding

Sound Memories

Directions: A useful technique for learning new words is to use multiple *senses.* For instance, by reading the vocabulary list, you used your sense of sight. In this activity, you'll use your sense of hearing to further study the words. Here's what to do:

1. Form a group of five people. Assign two vocabulary words to each of you.

2. On your own, do two things for each of your words.

   a. Divide the word into syllables. (A dictionary can help.)

   b. Practice saying the word aloud. (You may wish to check your pronunciation with a teacher or an online dictionary with audio.) Pay attention to which syllable is stressed. Make sure you *enunciate* precisely. For example, don't slur syllables together, don't drop a sound that should be spoken, and don't say an *m* sound when it should be an *n* sound.

3. Regroup and take turns doing these two things:

   a. Speak each of your words aloud, enunciating carefully.

   b. Pause after each word. Ask your listeners to write the word, spelling it as they hear it. Ask them to write an accent mark over the stressed syllable.

4. Regroup with the entire class. Share insights and ask questions. Perhaps, before this activity, you pronounced *postpone* as "pospone," leaving out the *t.* Or perhaps you discovered that some people pronounce *semiconscious* with a long *i* sound, and some people pronounce it with a long *e* sound.

Link It: Make Word-to-World Connections

Rhythm

Directions: In this activity, you'll work alone or with a partner to create a rap, rhyme, or chant. Follow these steps:

1. Choose a rhythmic pattern to use. Examples include a military cadence such as "I don't know what you've been told," the rhythm of a familiar rap, and the singsong pattern of a nursery rhyme such as "Twinkle, Twinkle, Little Star."

2. Play around with the vocabulary words, forming phrases or sentences and setting them to the rhythm. You can be light-hearted, goofy, serious, thoughtful—it's up to you. Use as many of the vocabulary words as you can. You can also use words that you wrote in the prefix wheels earlier in this chapter.

3. Perform your creation for the class.

Master It: Use Words in Meaningful Ways

Making Sense

Directions: In this lesson, you used your senses of sight and hearing to study the vocabulary words. Now think of all five senses: sight, hearing, taste, touch, smell. Which sense(s) could you use to further explore a specific vocabulary word?

For example, focus on *sight* by using maps related to the Mexican War (also called the Mexican-American War) to learn how national boundaries changed *postwar*.

Or use *taste* to contrast the products of a skilled cook and a *semiskilled* cook.

Get the idea? Use your imagination to generate ideas for connecting vocabulary words and one of the five senses. Then carry out *one* idea by linking a vocabulary word with a sense. Finally, share the results with your class.

List 3   Words with Greek Prefixes

You've studied two sets of Latin prefixes. Now here are four Greek prefixes and words that are formed with them. Read each word, what it means, and how it's used.

Prefix	Meaning	Examples
anti-	against	**anti**biotic, **anti**dote, **anti**septic
epi-	upon; over	**epi**demic, **epi**logue, **epi**taph
mon-, mono-	one	**mono**logue, **mono**rail
poly-	many; much	**poly**gon, **poly**syllabic

Word	What It Means	How It's Used
antibiotic *(n)* an-tee-by-AH-tik	a substance that destroys germs, used to treat diseases	The doctor prescribed an *antibiotic* to fight the patient's infection.
antidote *(n)* AN-ti-doht	a remedy to counteract the effects of a poison	The label on the bottle identifies an *antidote* to be given in case of accidental poisoning.
antiseptic *(n)* an-tuh-SEP-tik	a substance that fights germs so as to prevent infection	After you thoroughly wash a cut, you should apply an *antiseptic*.
epidemic *(n)* eh-pih-DEH-mik	a rapidly spreading disease that affects a large number of people (from *epi-* + *demos*, "people")	Doctors administered a vaccine in hopes of preventing a flu *epidemic*.
epilogue *(n)* EH-puh-lawg	a concluding section added to a novel or other literary work, providing additional information	In the book's *epilogue*, the novelist briefly tells what happens to the story's main characters in the future.
epitaph *(n)* EH-pih-taf	an inscription on a gravestone in memory of the person buried there	The *epitaph* on this tomb includes a famous line of poetry.
monologue *(n)* MAH-nuh-lawg	a long speech made by one speaker	The comedian's *monologue* drew laughter and applause from the audience.
monorail *(n)* MAH-nuh-rale	a railway in which cars operate on a single rail	Passengers ride a *monorail* from the parking lot to the airport terminal.

continued

| polygon *(n)* PAH-lee-gahn | a closed plane figure having three or more sides and angles | A rectangle is one kind of *polygon*. |
| polysyllabic *(adj)* pah-lee-si-LAH-bik | having several syllables | The speaker used *polysyllabic* words in an effort to impress listeners. |

Own It: Develop Your Word Understanding

Prefix Matchup

Directions: In this activity, you will be given a prefix *or* a base word or root. Your job is to find a classmate who has the other half of your word. Here's how the activity works:

1. Your teacher will write each vocabulary word on an index card, then cut the cards in half so that the prefix is on one half and the base word or root is on the other half. Finally, your teacher will jumble the cards together in a box.

2. Each student chooses one card from the box.

3. Move around the classroom to find the person who has the other half of your word. When you find that person, practice saying the complete word aloud. Write the word on a sheet of paper and review the word's meaning. You and your partner should also write a sample sentence using your word.

4. As a pair, share your results with the class. One of you reads the word aloud to the class and states the word's meaning. The other one reads your sample sentence.

Link It: Make Word-to-World Connections

Now and Later

Directions: In this activity, you'll think about words you're learning now, and how these words may come in handy later. Pair up with a classmate and follow these steps:

1. One of you reads the first vocabulary word aloud. Together, make sure that you understand the meaning of the word.

2. On a sheet of paper, write the word. Then write an example of when or how you might use this word in the future.

3. Repeat steps 1 and 2 for each word in the list.

4. In a class discussion, share some of your results. Point out any words that you don't see yourself using in the future—and be surprised and informed by how others *do* plan to use the words!

In a play we're reading in English class, the main character's <u>monologues</u> are always filled with <u>polysyllabic</u> words that are hard to comprehend. But I don't despair; I use my knowledge of word parts to figure them out!

Master It: Use Words in Meaningful Ways

Here's an Example

Directions: In this activity, you'll link a vocabulary word to an example of that word in real life. Then you'll share this connection with your class as a means of teaching the word's meaning. Follow these steps:

1. Choose *one* vocabulary word to work with and identify an example of this word in real life. For instance, what is a common kind of *antibiotic*? What is an example of a book that includes an *epilogue*?

2. Prepare an oral presentation of about *2–4 minutes* based on your vocabulary word. For instance, you might explain what a *monologue* is and then read a short monologue from a play. You might explain what a *polygon* is and then draw examples. You might give a lesson in first aid, including the use of an *antiseptic*.

3. Present your oral presentation to the class.

List 4   Words with Anglo-Saxon Prefixes

Study these four Anglo-Saxon prefixes and the list of words that follows. Read each word, what it means, and how it's used.

Prefix	Meaning	Examples
a-	on; in; in a state	**a**blaze, **a**drift
fore-	before; earlier	**fore**boding, **fore**most, **fore**sight
out-	go beyond; exceed; surpass	**out**last, **out**maneuver, **out**spoken
up-	in or to a higher position or level	**up**heaval, **up**roar

Word	What It Means	How It's Used
ablaze *(adv)* uh-BLAYZ	on fire; burning	Sparks from the fireplace set the curtain *ablaze*.
adrift *(adv)* uh-DRIFT	floating freely; drifting	With our raft *adrift* on the lake, we lay back and looked up at the clouds.
foreboding *(n)* fawr-BOH-ding	a sign or feeling of something evil or harmful to come	I took one look at the old gray house and was filled with *foreboding*.
foremost *(adj)* FAWR-mohst	leading; most important	Mr. Steger is the nation's *foremost* authority on air travel.
foresight *(n)* FAWR-site	careful or wise thought regarding the future	Thanks to your *foresight*, we have enough firewood to last us through the winter.
outlast *(v)* out-LAST	to keep going or last longer than	Because the tennis player was in peak condition, she was able to *outlast* her opponents.
outmaneuver *(v)* out-muh-NOO-ver	to plan or perform with greater skill	The driver *outmaneuvered* the other racers and finished in first place.
outspoken *(adj)* out-SPOH-kuhn	speaking out boldly and freely, without reserve	Emily is very *outspoken* and hurt Sarah's feelings when she criticized her outfit.
upheaval *(n)* up-HEE-vuhl	severe or sudden disturbance or disorder	The dictator's actions caused political *upheaval* in the country.
uproar *(n)* UP-rawr	a state of commotion or noisy disturbance	Fans were in an *uproar* when their first-place team lost to the worst team in the league.

Own It: Develop Your Word Understanding

Talking in Class

Directions: Work with a partner to complete the activity. Here's what to do:

1. Your teacher will assign you and your partner one vocabulary word. You then do three things:

   a. Identify the word's prefix and practice saying the word aloud.

   b. Express the word's meaning using your own words.

   c. Think of one other word (not in the vocabulary list) that uses the same prefix.

2. Your teacher will ask you and your partner to present your word to the class. Do three things:

   a. Pronounce the word and then state what the prefix is.

   b. Explain the word's meaning.

   c. Give an example of another word that uses the same prefix.

Link It: Make Word-to-World Connections

It's All in Your Head

Directions: Work with a partner to complete the activity. Follow the four steps:

1. Read the headings in the table below.

2. Your partner reads each vocabulary word aloud. After you hear each word, write it in one of the columns in the table.

This word is new to me in this lesson.	I have heard this word, but I've never used it.	I have used this word before.

3. Repeat step 2. This time, you read the words aloud to your partner.

4. Compare lists. Talk about when you have heard these words before and how you have used them. Read the words in the first column aloud to help them become more familiar.

Master It: Use Words in Meaningful Ways

Five-Minute Mastery

Directions: In this activity, you'll write very quickly for five minutes about *one* vocabulary word. Here's how the activity works:

1. Choose one vocabulary word.

2. Get out a sheet of paper and set a timer for five minutes. (Your teacher may watch the time for you.) Begin by writing the first thought in your head about the vocabulary word. This thought could be a definition, a sentence using the word, a memory inspired by the word, or any other thought. There is no "wrong" thing to write.

3. Keep writing. Don't stop! Write descriptions, statements, questions, lines of poetry, phrases, facts, opinions, and anything else. Let one thought lead into the next.

4. After five minutes, stop writing.

5. Silently, read what you wrote. Then, in a class discussion, share an interesting idea or thought from your writing. Finally, take a moment to feel satisfaction with your five-minute mastery of the vocabulary word.

rapping Up: Review What You've Learned

Here's a brief summary of what you've studied in this chapter.

> A **base word** is a complete word to which word parts may be added. A **root** is a word part from which other words are formed. A root is different from a base word because a root usually cannot stand by itself.

> A **prefix** is a group of letters added to the *beginning* of a base word or root so as to create a new word. A **suffix** is a group of letters added to the *end* of a base word or root so as to create a new word.

> Most prefixes in the English language come from Latin, Greek, or Anglo-Saxon (Old English).

> Every prefix has its own meaning. A prefix may have just one meaning, or it may have more than one. Different prefixes can have the same meaning.

> Some prefixes are spelled in more than one way.

> Some words put two prefixes together.

> Recognizing prefixes and understanding their meaning can help you figure out the meaning of words.

> Often you can figure out the meaning of an unfamiliar word by combining your knowledge of the word's prefix with clues from the *context*, or surrounding words.

> You've learned the following sixteen prefixes and words that are made with them. Can you remember what each prefix means? Page numbers are listed so you can check the answer if you're not sure.

ad- (page 5)	semi- (page 10)	a- (page 16)
circum- (page 5)	super- (page 10)	fore- (page 16)
contra- (page 5)	anti- (page 13)	out- (page 16)
e-, ex- (page 5)	epi- (page 13)	up-(page 16)
im-, in, ir- (page 10)	mon-, mono- (page 13)	
post- (page 10)	poly- (page 13)	

Chapter Review Exercises

Flaunt It: Show Your Word Understanding

In the following exercises, you'll demonstrate your understanding of each vocabulary word. You will use vocabulary words, or forms of the words, to complete sentences and to write sentences of your own.

A Word Bank

Directions: Choose a word from the box to complete each sentence. Write the word on the line provided. Each word may be used only once.

> irrelevant   ablaze   adhere   adrift   semiconscious
> polysyllabic   adjacent   postpone   extract   semiskilled

1. Sam's and Olivia's houses are _____ to each other.

2. Lying in a pool of sunshine, the drowsy puppy was only _____.

3. Please _____ to the rules of behavior while in the museum.

4. The nurse used tweezers to _____ the splinter from Noah's finger.

5. In this report on reptiles, the paragraph about starfish is _____.

6. Unfortunately, we must _____ the museum field trip until next month.

7. Highly skilled workers are usually paid more money than _____ workers.

8. Mrs. Pope said, "All but one word in the spelling list is _____."

9. Did you hear that last night, a bolt of lightning set the hillside _____?

10. Look at that helium-filled balloon _____ in the air!

B   Sentence Completion

Directions: Circle the letter of the word that best completes each sentence.

11. When my brother scraped his knee, I offered to apply a/an _____ to the injury.

    a. antiseptic
    c. contraband
    b. epidemic
    d. antidote

12. The shoplifter was _____ from the store, but charges were not filed.

    a. contradicted
    c. ejected
    b. outmaneuvered
    d. eluded

13. At the end of her e-mail, after her name, Heather added a/an _____.

    a. epitaph
    c. monologue
    b. postscript
    d. epilogue

14. Do you know how to determine the _____ of a circle?

    a. superficial
    c. circumference
    b. polygon
    d. circumnavigate

15. After making numerous questionable calls, the umpire was fired from his job because he was _____.

    a. foremost
    c. semiconscious
    b. supernatural
    d. incompetent

C   Writing

Directions: Follow the directions to write sentences using vocabulary words. Write your sentences on a separate sheet of paper.

16. Use *advocate* to make a statement about something you support or believe in.

17. Use *immortal* in a sentence about a character from literature.

18. Use *postwar* in a question about World War II.

19. Use *antibiotic* in a question to a nurse.

20. Use *monorail* to tell about transportation.

21. Use *foreboding* to tell how you felt in a certain situation.

22. Use *foresight* in a statement about a friend or family member.

23. Use *outlast* to describe a competition.

24. Use *upheaval* in a statement about a disaster.

25. Use *uproar* to tell about a crowd of people.

Chapter Extension Activities

Activities à la Carte: Extend Your Word Knowledge

The activities on this page are presented à la carte, like items on a restaurant menu, meaning that you can choose from a variety of options. Your teacher may assign an activity or let you pick the one that tempts your appetite. If time allows, you might do more than one activity. All of the activities feature the same ingredient: **prefixes**. Dig in!

Fashion Forward

Fashion trends come and go, and they often can be surprising, shocking, classy, or just plain funny. Use prefixes in this chapter to inspire your own fashion designs, complete with the name for the designer label and "verbiage" to print on the clothing items. If you're verbally creative but can't draw well (or vice versa), team up with someone who complements your skills. Then unveil your fashion line to the class.

Do the Math

Polygon is just one example of a mathematical term that uses a prefix. What are other examples? Create a lesson that teaches math terms—some using prefixes, some without—suitable for your classmates. Choose a format that fits your "teaching style"— a poster, a Web site, a videotaped presentation, or something else. Then get permission to teach your lesson in English class, in math class, or both.

Career Insights

Choose a career that interests you and examine specialized terms linked to that career. You might, for instance, look at medicine, the law, mathematics, theater, or transportation, to name a few. Begin by identifying vocabulary words from this chapter that connect to that career. Then, using those prefixes as a starting point, identify other words—with and without prefixes—used in that career. Create a summary of your research (such as a table of words, meanings, and examples of use) to display in class.

Yes, I Am Bilingual

Choose ten words from this chapter and translate them into another language. Create a three-column table like those in this chapter and fill in the information in the second language. Finally, compare the English words and information with the translated material. What conclusions can you draw? For instance, do both languages use the same prefixes? Can you translate a word *with* a prefix in English into a word *without* a prefix in the second language? Could having knowledge of prefixes help someone learn this language?

Adrift Without You

Use your knowledge of prefixes to write an irresistible invitation to a friend or to someone you want to be friends with. Is your *foremost* desire to have a party with that person there? Does *foresight* tell you that the two of you are destined for great things together? Are differences between you *irrelevant*? Use your own ideas to write a note. Deliver it and await a response.

Beyond Five Minutes

Did you enjoy the Five-Minute Mastery activity (page 18)? Then extend the experience! Use vocabulary words and ideas in your writing to inspire another dimension of expression. Perhaps you can use your ideas about *ablaze* to craft a poem or to inspire a painting. Perhaps your ideas about *uproar* will lead to a stunning photograph or a haunting melody. As an added challenge, insert the key word in your new creation.

Revise Your World

Have you ever noticed that road signs and other types of "environmental print" use simple, basic words? For a week, take note of signs, banners, billboards, and other print on display. Then choose a few examples to make over using vivid vocabulary words. A "Detour" sign could be revised to read "To *outmaneuver* the *upheaval*, use *adjacent* street." Your new verbiage may not fit on the original signs, but your words will certainly be captivating!

Learning Words Through Suffixes

2

I n Chapter 1, you learned how to "recycle" words by adding prefixes to base words and roots to form new words. Another way to reuse base words and roots is by adding a suffix. A **suffix** is a word part added to the end of a base word or root to create a new word. For instance, by adding -*er* to *manage*, you create *manager*. You can recycle *manager* by adding -*ment* to form *management*.

In this chapter, you'll continue your study of word parts by looking closely at suffixes. You'll learn a variety of common suffixes and practice using words that end with those suffixes.

Objectives

In this chapter, you will learn

> What a suffix is
> How and why to add suffixes
> Words with noun, verb, adjective, and adverb suffixes

Sneak Peek: Preview the Lesson

What I Know Already

Are you able to tell whether a word has a suffix? Test your suffix-recognition skills by sorting the words in the box at the top of the next page. Write each word that has *no* suffix in the first column. Write each word that *does* have a suffix in the second column. In the third column, write additional words that you can think of that have suffixes.

After you finish this chapter, return to this activity. Check your work and make any necessary corrections using your new knowledge.

Word Box

partnership	fixate	restive	berry
prize	convenience	freeway	historic
inspire	heavily	digitize	soften

Words without Suffixes	Words with Suffixes	Other Words I Know with Suffixes

Vocabulary Mini-Lesson: All About Suffixes

What Is a Suffix?

While prefixes are word parts attached to the *beginning* of words, suffixes are word parts attached to the *end*. Specifically, a **suffix** is a group of letters added to the end of a base word or root so as to create a new word.

Each suffix has its own meaning. For example, the suffix *-less* means "without." When you add *-less* to the following base words, what new words are formed?

BASE WORD	+	SUFFIX	=	WORD
thought	+	*-less*	=	*thoughtless*

Your <u>thoughtless</u> comment hurt my feelings.

BASE WORD	+	SUFFIX	=	WORD
meaning	+	*-less*	=	*meaningless*

A rule that is not enforced is <u>meaningless</u>.

The suffix *-ful* has the opposite meaning of *-less*. It means "full of" or "having." Let's add *-ful* to those same base words.

BASE WORD	+	SUFFIX	=	WORD
thought	+	*-ful*	=	*thoughtful*

Thank you for giving me such <u>thoughtful</u> advice.

BASE WORD	+	SUFFIX	=	WORD
meaning	+	*-ful*	=	*meaningful*

Helping other people is a <u>meaningful</u> activity.

You can see how adding different suffixes to the same base word creates new words with very different meanings.

Suffixes are similarly added to roots. Often, you can add a variety of suffixes to the same root. For example, the suffix *-ate* means "to make." Let's add it to the Latin root *liber*, which means "free."

ROOT	+	SUFFIX	=	WORD
liber	+	*-ate*	=	*liberate* (*to make* free)

Soldiers <u>liberated</u> the captives from prison.

Now let's add a different suffix to the same root. The suffix *-ty* means "condition of being."

liber	+	*-ty*	=	*liberty* (*condition of being* free)

Americans celebrate their <u>liberty</u> on the Fourth of July.

In the same way, you can combine the root *liber* with the suffixes *-al* and *-ation* to form the words *liberal* and *liberation*. You'll learn more about roots in Chapter 3.

> ## Tip
>
> Keep in mind that many words contain more than one suffix. Here are some examples.
>
> *fearlessness* = fear + *-less* + *-ness*
>
> *delightfully* = delight + *-ful* + *-ly*
>
> What others can you think of?

Why Learn This?

Learning suffixes can help your reading comprehension. Suffixes often give you a clue about a word's part of speech, and knowing a word's part of speech can help you understand a sentence you're reading. For example, words ending in the suffix *-ment* are usually nouns. *Embarrass<u>ment</u>* and *develop<u>ment</u>* are two examples. Similarly, many words ending in *-ly* are adverbs. *Triumphant<u>ly</u>* and *vigorous<u>ly</u>* are examples.

When you know a word's part of speech, you can see how the word relates to other words in the sentence. This helps you understand the sentence better. Look at these examples.

We could tell by the *jubilant* expression on Hannah's face that she had done well on the exam.
(*Jubilant* is an adjective, describing Hannah's expression.)

"I got an A on the test!" Hannah said *jubilantly*.
(*Jubilantly* is an adverb, describing how Hannah was speaking.)

Even if you didn't know what *jubilantly* means, you could use your knowledge of the suffix *-ly* to figure out that it's an adverb describing how Hannah was speaking. This helps you figure out what it means.

Quick Review: The Parts of Speech

Suffixes help you identify these parts of speech:

Noun names a person, place, thing, or idea

Examples: *mayor, continent, computer, freedom*

Verb usually expresses action

Examples: *crawl, whisper, examine*

Adjective describes a noun or a pronoun

Examples: *broad, green, harsh*

Adverb usually describes a verb but may also describe an adjective or another adverb

Examples: *swiftly, precisely*

Words to Know: Vocabulary Lists and Activities

In Chapter 1, prefixes were grouped according to their language of origin: Latin, Greek, or Anglo-Saxon. Suffixes too come from different languages, and many English words combine suffixes from one language with roots and prefixes from other languages. Rather than focus on their origin, this chapter groups suffixes by the part of speech they usually show: noun, verb, adjective, and adverb.

Just as with prefixes, keep several points in mind.

> A suffix may have more than one meaning. For example, the noun suffix *-ness* can refer to a "quality" *or* a "condition." Compare these sentences:

The chess champion was praised for his *cleverness.*

(the *quality* of being clever)

The accident victim regained *consciousness* in the hospital.

(the *condition* of being conscious)

> Different suffixes can have the same meaning. For instance, the suffixes *-en* and *-ize* both mean "to make," as in *sharpen* and *legalize.*

> Adding a suffix can change a word from one part of speech to another.

From verb to noun:	govern + *-ment* = government
From adjective to verb:	weak + *-en* = weaken
From noun to adjective:	sense + *-less* = senseless
From adjective to adverb:	accurate + *-ly* = accurately

> Some suffixes are spelled in more than one way. For example, *-ant* and *-ent* are two forms of the same suffix, meaning "being or acting in a certain way," as in *defiant* and *persistent*.

> When a suffix is added to a base word, the word may stay the same, or letters may be dropped, added, or changed. Here are a few examples.

defense + *-less* = defense*less* (no spelling change)

debate + *-able* = debat*able* (the *e* is dropped)

easy + *-ly* = easi*ly* (*y* changes to *i*)

You'll learn more about such spelling changes in Chapter 4.

List 5   Words with Noun Suffixes

Study these four noun suffixes and the list of words (nouns) that contain them. Read each word, what it means, and how it's used.

Suffix	Meaning	Examples
-ance, -ence	state, quality, or process	belliger**ence**, guid**ance**, radi**ance**
-ation, -ion	action, state, or condition	expect**ation**, inspir**ation**, tens**ion**
-ism	behavior characteristic of; also, doctrine or system	commun**ism**, hero**ism**
-ship	quality or state of being	owner**ship**, statesman**ship**

Word	What It Means	How It's Used
belligerence *(n)* buh-LIJ-er-runts	aggressively hostile attitude; hostility	The *belligerence* of the dictator led to war with neighboring nations.
guidance *(n)* GUY-dunts	process of guiding; direction	With his teacher's *guidance*, Ethan improved his writing skills.

continued

radiance *(n)* RAY-dee-uhns	the state or quality of being radiant, or bright	The *radiance* of the distant star made it easy to see.
expectation *(n)* ek-spek-TAY-shuhn	act or state of expecting; anticipation	My *expectation* of how the movie would end proved correct.
inspiration *(n)* in-spuh-RAY-shuhn	something that inspires; a stimulating or motivating influence	The artist found *inspiration* in Arizona's magnificent landscapes.
tension *(n)* TEN-shuhn	tense state or condition; stress; anxiety	With only two minutes left in the game, everyone could feel the *tension* in the air.
communism *(n)* KOM-yuh-nih-zuhm	economic system under which property is owned by the community as a whole	The spread of *communism* marked the beginning of the so-called cold war between the Soviet Union and the United States.
heroism *(n)* HER-uh-wih-zuhm	the behavior or qualities of a hero	Mayor Lindsey praised the firefighters for their *heroism* in rescuing the children from the burning building.
ownership *(n)* OH-ner-ship	the state or fact of being an owner	Michael has a bill of sale to prove his *ownership* of the car.
statesmanship *(n)* STAYTS-muhn-ship	the qualities, abilities, or methods of a statesman; skill in handling public affairs	Communication and leadership skills are key aspects of *statesmanship*.

Own It: Develop Your Word Understanding

Suffix Organizers

Directions: For each graphic organizer, follow these steps:

1. *Top:* Read the suffix or suffixes in the top box.
2. *Middle:* In the "used in" box, write the vocabulary words that use the given suffix or suffixes. In the "meaning" box, write the meaning of the suffix or suffixes. In the "memory cue" box, sketch or write a clue to help you remember the suffix's meaning.
3. *Bottom*: Use your knowledge of each key word to complete the sentences.
4. Finally, pair up with a classmate to share your work and get help, if needed. Based on your discussion, add notes or corrections to your organizers.

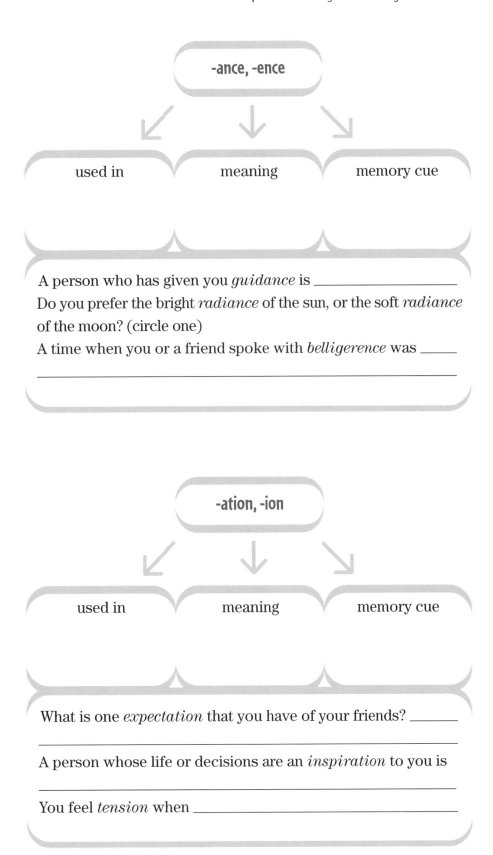

-ance, -ence

| used in | meaning | memory cue |

A person who has given you *guidance* is _____

Do you prefer the bright *radiance* of the sun, or the soft *radiance* of the moon? (circle one)

A time when you or a friend spoke with *belligerence* was _____

_____

-ation, -ion

| used in | meaning | memory cue |

What is one *expectation* that you have of your friends? _____

_____

A person whose life or decisions are an *inspiration* to you is

_____

You feel *tension* when _____

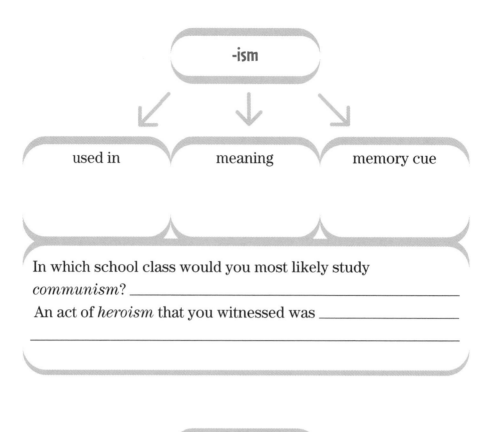

In which school class would you most likely study *communism*? _____

An act of *heroism* that you witnessed was _____

_____

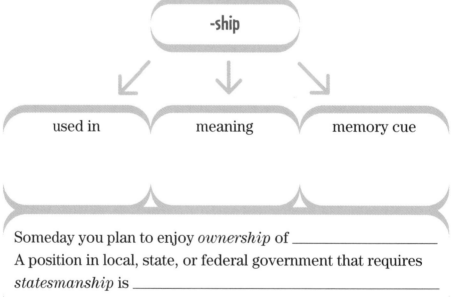

Someday you plan to enjoy *ownership* of _____

A position in local, state, or federal government that requires *statesmanship* is _____

Link It: Make Word-to-World Connections

All About Us

Directions: Your assignment is to create a poster about your family or your "family" of friends. Here's what to do:

1. Study the list of vocabulary words. Think about ways these words connect to you and your family or friends. Perhaps you can use the words *to inform* (give information), *to entertain* (tell amusing facts or stories), *to describe* (give details to create a mental image), or *to persuade* (convince readers to share your view of your family). Write phrases and sentences using the vocabulary words.

2. Add some visual appeal. Gather art supplies, photographs, mementos (such as baseball cards or ticket stubs), and other materials to bring your poster to life.

3. Put it all together. Arrange the sentences and phrases from step 1 on the poster, and use the materials from step 2 to make the project eye-catching.

4. Share your poster with your family, friends, and classmates.

Master It: Use Words in Meaningful Ways

Abstract Exhibit

Directions: Each noun in the vocabulary list is an *abstract noun*. This means you can't touch it, taste it, smell it, or use other senses to experience it.

Even though each noun is abstract, you probably have mental images linked to some of the words. For example, *tension* may make you picture the frown lines on a parent's forehead. *Ownership* may bring to mind a photograph of your friend and his new dirt bike. These mental images help you make sense of abstract nouns.

In this activity, you'll explore one abstract noun. Here's what to do:

1. Review the vocabulary words, thinking about mental images that they inspire. Choose one word for this project.

2. Write a paragraph describing the image that the key word brings to mind. For a powerful paragraph, give details that appeal to various senses (touch, taste, smell, hearing, sight).

3. Find or create a picture that is the same as or similar to the mental image you described in step 2.

4. On paper or poster board, attach the picture and the paragraph. Display your project in a class Abstract Exhibit.

List 6   Words with Verb Suffixes

The last list contained noun suffixes; now you'll focus on some verb suffixes. Study the suffixes and the ten words (verbs) that contain them. Read each word, what it means, and how it's used.

Suffix	Meaning	Examples
-ate	to cause to be or become; make	captiv**ate**, evacu**ate**, infuri**ate**
-en	to cause to be or become; make	embold**en**, heart**en**
-fy	to cause to be or become; make	forti**fy**, mysti**fy**, veri**fy**
-ize	to cause to be or become; make	fanta**size**, immun**ize**

Word	What It Means	How It's Used
captivate (v) KAP-tuh-vate	to influence through an irresistible appeal or attraction; capture the attention of	The young singer's wonderful voice *captivated* audiences around the world.
evacuate (v) i-VAH-kyuh-wait	to remove from	Police *evacuated* residents from the damaged building.
infuriate (v) in-FYOOR-ee-ate	to make angry; enrage	My cousin's insulting remark *infuriated* me.
embolden (v) em-BOHL-duhn	to make bold; fill with courage	The general feared that retreat would *embolden* the enemy.
hearten (v) HAHR-tn	to raise the spirits of; encourage	The unexpected good news *heartened* us.
fortify (v) FAWR-tuh-fie	to make strong; strengthen (from Latin *fortis*, meaning "strong")	Concrete barriers *fortified* the building against attack.
mystify (v) MIS-tuh-fie	to puzzle; bewilder; perplex	The magician's tricks *mystified* the children.

continued

verify *(v)* VER-uh-fie	to establish the accuracy or truth of; confirm (from Latin *verus*, meaning "true")	Please *verify* these facts by checking them in an encyclopedia.
fantasize *(v)* FAN-tuh-size	to imagine; daydream	Jordyn likes to *fantasize* what life would be like as a famous actress.
immunize *(v)* IH-myuh-nize	to make immune, as by vaccination	School officials urged parents to *immunize* their children against measles and other childhood diseases.

Own It: Develop Your Word Understanding

Suffix Wheels

Directions: Follow the steps to complete the activity.

1. Fill in each suffix wheel by writing the meaning of each word in the space provided.

2. In each empty section of a wheel, write an additional word that uses the given suffix, along with the meaning of the word.

3. Your teacher will call out someone's name and identify a suffix. That person reads one section in that suffix wheel. Then that person calls out someone else's name and identifies a suffix.

4. Continue calling out names and reading sections from wheels until four words for each wheel have been read. Take notes on words that other people suggest for each wheel.

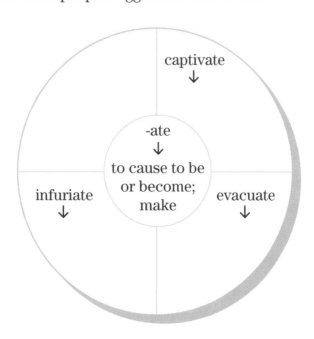

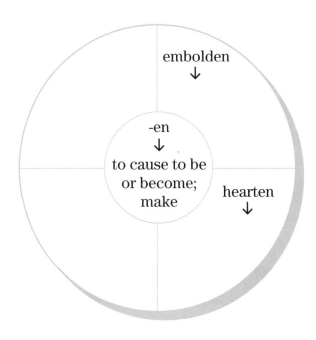

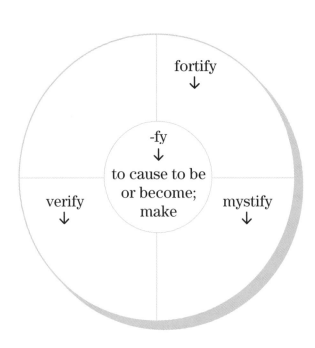

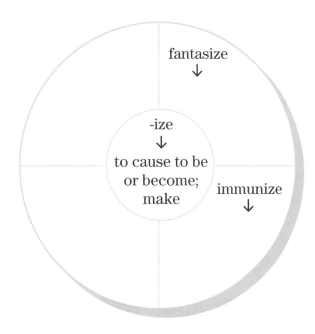

Link It: Make Word-to-World Connections

Let Me Explain

Directions: Can you explain how to *embolden* a shy friend? Or how students should *evacuate* the school in case of fire or emergency? Or how to *fantasize* your way to a winning football season? Think about how the verbs in the vocabulary list relate to something you know how to do. Then follow these steps:

1. Write a few sentences that explain how to do something. You can be serious or funny. You can explain something that your friends know little about, or something that is familiar to many. The goal is to use *two or more* vocabulary words in your explanation.

2. Gather in small groups. Read your explanation aloud. Then ask group members to identify the vocabulary words used in your explanation. Ask them if they can suggest yet another vocabulary word that would fit in your explanation.

Master It: Use Words in Meaningful Ways

Critic's Choice

Directions: In this activity, you'll become an "entertainment critic" and write a review for your classmates. Here's what to do.

1. Choose a movie, book, or music album to review.

2. Watch the movie, read the book, or listen to the album. As you do so, takes notes on strong points, weak points, remarkable sections or ideas, and so on. Keep the vocabulary words handy and let them inspire some of your comments.

3. Write your review. A useful format to follow is to (1) introduce the item being reviewed, (2) describe several strong/positive qualities, (3) mention a need for improvement (if any), and (4) give your overall impression. (For instance, "This book will appeal to fans of extreme sports.") Aim for a reading time of *3–4 minutes.*

4. With your teacher, plan a Critic's Choice event in class, when you snack on popcorn while people share their reviews. Afterward, you'll have enough entertainment recommendations to keep you busy for a month!

List 7   Words with Adjective Suffixes

Here are some common adjective suffixes and ten words (adjectives) that are formed with them. Read each word, what it means, and how it's used.

Suffix	Meaning	Examples
-able, -ible	capable of being	access**ible**, invinc**ible**, notice**able**
-ic, -ical	like, relating to, or having the qualities of	diplomat**ic**, econom**ical**
-ive	relating to or inclined to	exhaus**tive**, fes**tive**, repeti**tive**
-ous	full of or having	amor**ous**, malici**ous**

Word	What It Means	How It's Used
accessible *(adj)* ik-SEH-suh-buhl	capable of being reached or entered	The cabin in the woods is *accessible* only on foot.
invincible *(adj)* in-VIN-suh-buhl	not capable of being conquered; unbeatable (See *in-* on List 2, page 10.)	No team in the league could defeat the Falcons last year; they were *invincible*.
noticeable *(adj)* NOH-ti-suh-buhl	easily noticed; clear; obvious	Having a math tutor has made a *noticeable* difference in William's grades.
diplomatic *(adj)* dih-pluh-MAH-tik	having to do with relations between nations	The president sent his representative on a *diplomatic* mission to China.
economical *(adj)* eh-kuh-NAH-mi-kuhl	making wise use of resources; not wasteful	Our *economical* new car gets nearly twice as many miles to the gallon as our old one did.
exhaustive *(adj)* ig-ZAW-stiv	thorough; comprehensive (See *ex-* on List 1, page 5.)	After doing an *exhaustive* study of the medication, scientists summarized their conclusions in a detailed report.
festive *(adj)* FES-tiv	suitable for a festival or celebration	The colorful decorations and lively music create a *festive* atmosphere.
repetitive *(adj)* ri-PEH-ti-tiv	tending to repeat	The lyrics of this song are so *repetitive* that they soon become boring.
amorous *(adj)* AH-meh-ruhs	relating to or showing love (from Latin *amor*, meaning "love")	The couple exchanged many *amorous* smiles at their wedding.
malicious *(adj)* muh-LIH-shuhs	intentionally hurtful; mean	Spreading a false rumor is a *malicious* thing to do.

Own It: Develop Your Word Understanding

Exploring Key Words

Directions: Use the following graphic organizers to explore word parts and word meanings. Work with a partner to complete the steps.

1. Pronounce the key word aloud.

2. In the first box, divide the word into syllables. Place an accent mark over the stressed syllable. (A dictionary can help.)

3. Review the word's definition. Then, with your partner, form a definition in your own words. Write it in the second box.

4. In the bottom box, write an example of how or when you have seen/heard the word used. If you want, write several examples. These examples will help you remember the word's meaning.

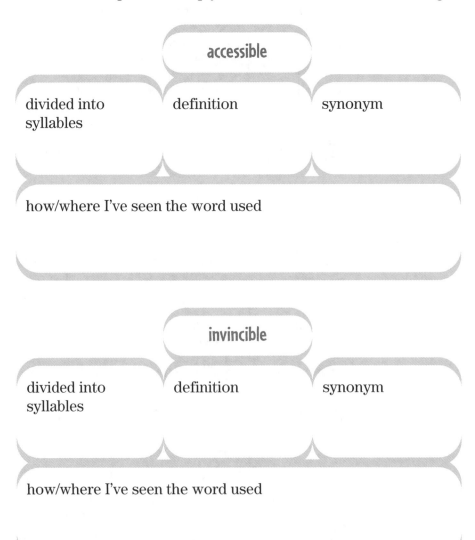

accessible

| divided into syllables | definition | synonym |

how/where I've seen the word used

invincible

| divided into syllables | definition | synonym |

how/where I've seen the word used

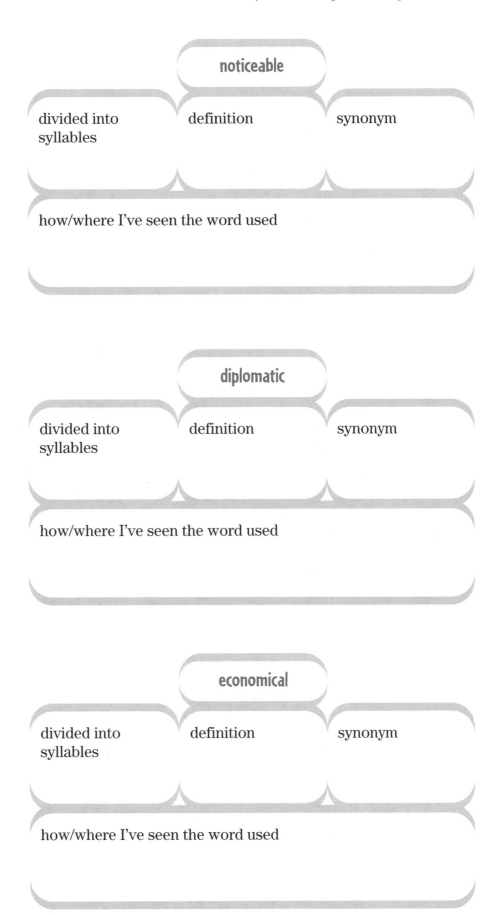

noticeable

| divided into syllables | definition | synonym |

how/where I've seen the word used

diplomatic

| divided into syllables | definition | synonym |

how/where I've seen the word used

economical

| divided into syllables | definition | synonym |

how/where I've seen the word used

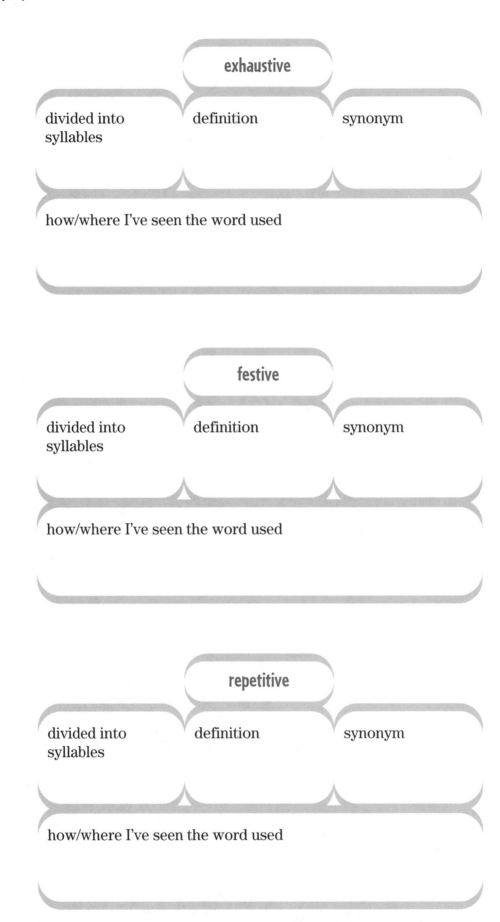

exhaustive

divided into syllables

definition

synonym

how/where I've seen the word used

festive

divided into syllables

definition

synonym

how/where I've seen the word used

repetitive

divided into syllables

definition

synonym

how/where I've seen the word used

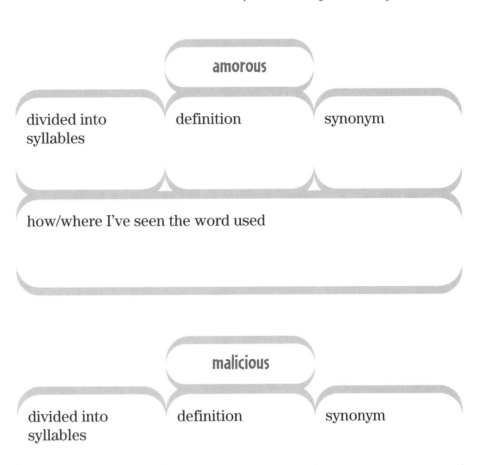

amorous

| divided into syllables | definition | synonym |

how/where I've seen the word used

malicious

| divided into syllables | definition | synonym |

how/where I've seen the word used

link it

Link It: Make Word-to-World Connections

Person, Place, or Thing?

Directions: Each word in the vocabulary list is an adjective. This means that you can use the words to describe people, places, and things. Try using the words in the table on the next page. Follow these steps:

1. Read each word in the first column.

2. In the second column, use the word in a description of a person, place, or thing. Your description can be a phrase, a sentence, or even multiple sentences. Sample responses for two words are completed for you.

3. Share your favorite description in a class discussion.

Adjective	Adjective Used in a Description
accessible	My math teacher is accessible after school for help with homework.
invincible	invincible me! invincible superhero
accessible	
invincible	
noticeable	
diplomatic	
economical	
exhaustive	
festive	
repetitive	
amorous	
malicious	

Master It: Use Words in Meaningful Ways

Pick One

Directions: In this activity, you'll write a *fictional, biographical,* or *descriptive* sketch. (A *sketch* is a short piece of writing that, in this case, captures a person, place, or thing.) Here's what to do:

1. Pick one type of sketch to write: fictional, biographical, or descriptive. For topic ideas, review your work in the Person, Place, or Thing? activity, above.

2. **Research** information that you'll need to write your sketch. You might interview a person for a biographical sketch, read encyclopedia entries or a nonfiction book for a descriptive sketch, or review the structure of a short story for a fictional sketch. Ask a teacher or librarian for help with resources, if needed.

3. **Write** a 200- to 300-word sketch of the person, place, or thing. In your writing, use at least one vocabulary word.

4. **Exchange** papers with a writing partner to get feedback. Read each other's sketches and point out one strength and one weakness in the sketch. Help each other decide how to improve on the weakness.

5. **Write** the final copy of your sketch and submit it to your teacher.

List 8 Words with Adverb Suffixes

The last list in this chapter contains three adverb suffixes. These suffixes usually form adverbs—words that describe verbs, adjectives, or other adverbs. Study the suffixes and the list of words that contain them. Read each word, what it means, and how it's used.

Suffix	Meaning	Examples
-ly	in a certain way	attentive**ly**, habitual**ly**, scornful**ly**, sound**ly**, strategical**ly**
-ward	in the direction of	on**ward**, out**ward**, way**ward**
-wise	in the direction or way of	counterclock**wise**, like**wise**

Word	What It Means	How It's Used
attentively (adv) uh-TEN-tiv-lee	paying close attention; carefully; alertly	The teacher advised students to listen *attentively* as she read aloud.
habitually (adv) huh-BIH-chuh-lee	regularly, as though a habit; usually	Matthew needs to wear a watch because he is *habitually* late.
scornfully (adv) SKAWRN-fuh-lee	with feelings of hatred or disrespect	"After what you did, I can no longer call you my friend," she said *scornfully*.
soundly (adv) SOUND-lee	without trouble or interruption; with sensibility and good judgment	I used to be able to sleep *soundly*, but lately I've been tossing and turning with nervousness about my upcoming test.

continued

strategically *(adv)* struh-TEE-jih-klee	as part of a plan	Soldiers were *strategically* located around the fort to stand guard.
onward *(adv)* ON-werd	toward a point ahead; forward	Despite their weariness, the hikers continued to walk *onward*.
outward *(adj, adv)* OUT-werd	on or toward the outside	Daniel's *outward* calm hides his inner nervousness.
wayward *(adj, adv)* WAY-werd	going one's own way; unruly; willful	Abigail follows all the rules, unlike her *wayward* sister.
counterclockwise *(adv)* koun-ter-KLOK-wize	in the direction opposite to that in which the hands of a clock move	Turn the lid *counterclockwise* to open the pickle jar.
likewise *(adv)* LAHYK-wize	in the same manner; similarly	José smiled and removed his cap; his brother did *likewise*.

Own It: Develop Your Word Understanding

Suffix Matchup

Directions: In this activity, you will be given a base word or root *or* a suffix. Your job is to find a classmate who has the other half of your word. Follow these steps:

1. Your teacher will write each vocabulary word on an index card, then cut the cards in half so that the prefix and base word or root is on one half and the suffix is on the other half. Finally, your teacher will jumble the cards together in a box.

2. Each student chooses one card from the box.

3. Move around the classroom to find the person who has the other half of your vocabulary word. When you find that person, practice saying the complete word aloud. Write the complete word on a sheet of paper and review the word's meaning. *Bonus: Think of another word (not in the vocabulary list) that uses the same suffix.*

4. When everyone has found a word partner, share the results. One of you reads the word aloud and shows how the root or base word and the suffix are combined. The other person states the word's meaning. If you thought of another word that uses the same suffix, share it, too.

Link It: Make Word-to-World Connections

The Things You Do

Directions: Each word in the vocabulary list is an *adverb*. As you know, adverbs are used to describe verbs, adjectives, and other adverbs in sentences. In this activity, you'll focus on using adverbs to describe *verbs*. How could you use the vocabulary words to describe your own actions?

Fill in the table by using each adverb to describe something you do. Two examples are completed for you. After you complete the table, pair up with a partner. Review your tables together and make additions and changes as necessary.

Adverb	Something I Do That Could Be Described with This Adverb
attentively	I listen attentively to my coach.
habitually	I habitually do twenty sit-ups a day.
attentively	

continued

habitually	
scornfully	
soundly	
strategically	
onward	
outward	
wayward	
counterclockwise	
likewise	

Master It: Use Words in Meaningful Ways

You're a Poet

Directions: In this activity, you'll use vocabulary words to create a rhythmic poem. If you don't often write poetry, don't worry—you've already completed some of the work! Follow these steps:

1. First, assemble the lines in your poem. For each line, use one of the sentences you wrote in The Things You Do on pages 47–48. Use any order you want for the lines.

2. Revise the sentences so that each one begins with the adverb, like this:

> Attentively, I listen to my coach.

> Habitually, I do twenty sit-ups a day.

Using the adverbs in this way gives *parallel structure* to the lines in your poem.

3. Give your poem a title, such as "The Things I Do."

4. Give a copy of your poem to your teacher and share it with friends and family.

Tip

Many words have both prefixes and suffixes. For example, two of the words you learned in Chapter 1 were *extract* (List 1) and *incompetent* (List 2). Both words contain prefixes, but you can also add suffixes, such as these that you've studied in this chapter:

extract + *-able* = <u>extractable</u>

incompetent + *-ly* = <u>incompetently</u>

You'll learn more about words that have both prefixes and suffixes in Chapter 4.

Wrapping Up: Review What You've Learned

Here's a brief summary of what you've studied in this chapter.

> A **suffix** is a group of letters added to the end of a base word or root so as to create a new word. Many words have more than one suffix.

> Like prefixes, suffixes come from different languages. Many words in English combine suffixes from one language with roots and prefixes from other languages.

> Every suffix has its own meaning. Adding different suffixes to the same base word creates new words with different meanings.

> A suffix may have more than one meaning. Different suffixes can have the same meaning.

> Adding a suffix can change a word from one part of speech to another.

> Some suffixes are spelled in more than one way. When a suffix is added to a base word, the word may stay the same, or letters may be dropped, added, or changed.

> Suffixes help you identify a word's part of speech and see how the word relates to other words in the sentence.

> You have learned these suffixes and words formed from them. Can you remember what each suffix means? Page references have been provided so you can check the ones you're not sure about.

-ance, -ence (page 29)	-fy (page 34)	-ly (page 45)
-ation, -ion (page 29)	-ize (page 34)	-ward (page 45)
-ism (page 29)	-able, -ible (page 39)	-wise (page 45)
-ship (page 29)	-ic, -ical (page 39)	
-ate (page 34)	-ive (page 39)	
-en (page 34)	-ous (page 39)	

Flaunt It: Show Your Word Understanding

In the following exercises, you'll demonstrate your understanding of each vocabulary word. You will use vocabulary words, or forms of the words, to complete sentences and to write sentences of your own.

A Matching

Directions: Match the underlined word to its definition. Write the letter of the definition on the line provided.

_____ 1. The chef finds <u>inspiration</u> for new recipes in memories of his grandmother's Sunday dinners.

_____ 2. The swimming lessons seemed to <u>embolden</u> Charlie, and he was no longer afraid to go out with his dad in the canoe.

_____ 3. Due to urban sprawl, business complexes pushed <u>outward</u> into land that previously was farmed.

_____ 4. To turn on the cold water, turn the handle <u>counterclockwise</u>, meaning to the left.

_____ 5. Posting your sister's diary on the Internet was a <u>malicious</u> thing to do.

_____ 6. I do homework during the bus ride home, and it's an <u>economical</u> use of my time.

_____ 7. At this year's regional skateboard competition, Blue Dog Davis was <u>invincible</u>.

_____ 8. The girls' soccer team won at regionals; <u>likewise</u>, the boys' team was victorious.

_____ 9. The friends, firm believers in <u>communism</u>, pooled their

a. to make bold; fill with courage

b. in the direction opposite to that in which the hands of a clock move

c. not capable of being conquered; unbeatable

d. something that inspires; a stimulating or motivating influence

e. intentionally hurtful; mean

f. economic system under which property is owned by the community as a whole

g. to remove from

h. on or toward the outside

i. in the same manner; similarly

j. making wise use of resources; not wasteful

resources and founded a commune where they would all live together.

_____ **10.** When the levee broke, flooding caused many citizens to <u>evacuate</u> their homes.

B Sentence Completion

Directions: Circle the letter of the word that best completes each sentence.

11. Due to her _____, the mayor was reelected.
- **a.** expectation
- **b.** diplomatic
- **c.** belligerence
- **d.** statesmanship

12. I feared that my team would lose, but when we made two baskets in a row, I was _____.
- **a.** verified
- **b.** heartened
- **c.** mystified
- **d.** amorous

13. Cassandra _____ begins her morning with coffee and dry toast, while I always eat eggs and oatmeal.
- **a.** habitually
- **b.** scornfully
- **c.** attentively
- **d.** soundly

14. A copy of the Declaration of Independence is _____ online, so anyone with Internet access can easily find this historical document.
- **a.** accessible
- **b.** exhaustive
- **c.** strategically
- **d.** noticeable

15. If you continue to taunt that dog mercilessly, you are likely to _____ him.
- **a.** immunize
- **b.** captivate
- **c.** infuriate
- **d.** fortify

C Writing

Directions: Follow the directions to write sentences using vocabulary words. Write your sentences on a separate sheet of paper.

16. Use *onward* to tell how someone met a goal. (You may use more than one sentence in your explanation.)

17. Use *radiance* in a description of a party. (You may use more than one sentence in your description.)

18. Use *fantasize* and *heroism* in the same sentence.

19. Use *ownership* and *tension* in the same sentence.

20. Use *guidance* and *wayward* in the same sentence.

Activities à la Carte: Extend Your Word Knowledge

The activities on this page are presented à la carte, like items on a restaurant menu, meaning that you can choose from a variety of options. Your teacher may assign an activity or let you pick the one that tempts your appetite. If time allows, you might do more than one activity. All of the activities feature the same ingredient: **suffixes**. Dig in!

My Life as a Suffix

If you were a suffix, which type would you be? Do you, like noun suffixes, label things clearly? Or, like verb suffixes, do you bring action wherever you go? Perhaps you're a little bossy, like adverb suffixes (Do it *this* way). Or, like adjective suffixes, you enjoy answering questions (Which one? What kind? How many?). Create a poster or write a couple of paragraphs explaining which type of suffix best reflects you.

In Other Words

Do you speak a language other than English? Get out the sketch you wrote for the Pick One activity on page 44. Translate the sketch into a second language. What happens to the suffixes in words when you translate them? Do the translated words contain suffixes? Do the suffixes in the second language sound similar to the English versions? Share your translated sketch with someone who speaks the language.

Inside Scoop

Plan a family (or friend) newsletter to report events, achievements, inside jokes, upcoming plans, and more. First, create a feature called "In This Issue" to print on the first page. This is like a table of contents. List the titles of the articles that will be in the newsletter. In each title, use at least one word with a suffix. Next, write the articles. Finally, put everything together as a newsletter. Your family and friends will treasure the copies you give them!

Smart Aleck

Use suffixes to create your own slang words. Start by listing some words that you and your friends often use. Then play around with adding suffixes to morph them into unique words that have meaning to you and your pals. Write a copy of your slang dictionary, available only to your closest friends.

In the News

If you have access to a video recorder or a camera, create a news story about suffixes in your community. Working with a partner, film short segments in which you stand before a store sign, poster, or other printed item and report on the presence (or absence) of suffixes. If you are using a camera, photograph the signs and use the photographs in a "live" broadcast to your class.

Tell Me!

Find out what a dictionary can tell you about suffixes by looking up a few. If you use an online dictionary, type a hyphen before the suffix, as in *-ly*. Start by looking up a few suffixes taught in this lesson. Then look up some suffixes that weren't in this lesson, such as *-ant*, *-en*, and *-ful*. Enlighten your class with your findings.

Business or Pleasure?

What would you rather be reading instead of doing homework? Maybe a football playbook, love note, or graphic novel? Why not combine business with pleasure? Relax and read what you want to. Then jot down a list of words with suffixes appearing in what you read. Share the results with your class. Explain whether suffixes appeared rarely or frequently, and whether they were mostly one type (say, noun suffixes), or a mix of types.

Learning Words Through Roots

3

Objectives

In this chapter, you will learn

> What a root is
> Why you should know roots
> Words with Greek and Latin roots

Close your eyes and picture some plants and trees in your mind. What do you see? Stems, trunks, leaves, and twigs probably fill your field of vision. You may have pictured colorful blossoms or long green palm fronds. But did you picture any *roots*?

Roots often go unnoticed, whether they are the roots of plants or the roots of words. However, just like plant roots, word roots are essential. The root of a word gives the word its basic meaning. Other words parts, such as prefixes and suffixes, add to that meaning. But without the root, the word would be a jumble of unconnected parts.

In this chapter, you'll practice identifying roots of words and look at how roots give words meaning.

Sneak Peek: Preview the Lesson

Agree or Disagree?

Read each statement at the top of the next page and decide whether you agree or disagree with it. If you agree, write YES on the line under Before Reading. If you disagree, write NO on this line.

After you complete the chapter, return to this page and fill out the After Reading column. Notice whether new knowledge leads you to answer differently.

Before Reading	**After Reading**

_____ 1. A word can contain more than one root. _____

_____ 2. Several roots can have the same meaning. _____

_____ 3. A root can stand alone as a word. _____

_____ 4. Roots of English words can come from
  other languages. _____

_____ 5. A root always appears in the middle
  of a word. _____

Vocabulary Mini-Lesson: All About Roots

A **root** is a word part from which other words are formed. As you learned in Chapter 1, a root is different from a base word. A base word is a complete word and can stand alone. A root usually cannot stand alone as a word.

In Chapters 1 and 2, you saw examples of how roots are combined with prefixes and suffixes. What are the roots in the following words? With what word part is each root combined?

re-	+	*vis(e)* (see)	=	revise ("to see again")
re-	+	*cede* (go)	=	recede ("to go back")
clarus (clear)	+	*-fy*	=	clarify ("to make clear")
magnus (great)	+	*-fy*	=	magnify ("to make great or large")

Can you identify the roots and word parts in these related words: *revision, clarity, magnification*?

Why Learn This?

Like prefixes and suffixes, roots come from other languages, such as Greek and Latin. While a root by itself may not look familiar, if you learn its meaning, you will have an important clue to the meaning of every word built on that root.

In fact, some roots will help you understand a wide range of words in the same large "family." For instance, numerous words are built on forms of the Latin word *tenere*, which means "to hold." These familiar root forms include *ten, tain*, and *tin*.

The tree diagram shows some of the many words that come from *tenere*.

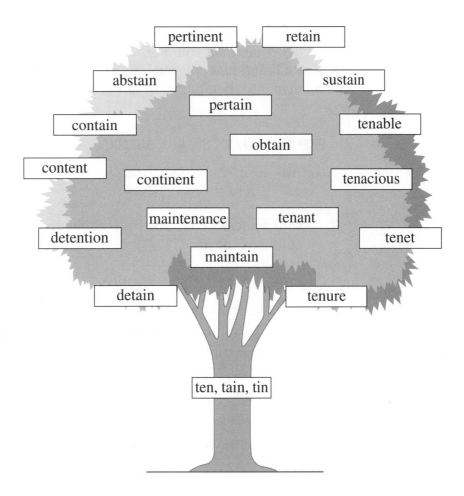

In what sense does each word in this word family relate to holding? Check a dictionary for definitions and word history if you're not sure. Can you suggest any words to add to the tree?

Tip

It's not always obvious at first glance how the parts of a word work together to give the word its meaning. Sometimes you have to really think about it. For example, in Chapter 1, you saw that the definition of *contradict* (*contra-* + *dict*) came from the literal meaning "to speak against." In Chapter 2, you saw that *verify*—which comes from the root *verus* (meaning "true") + the suffix *-fy*—means "to make true," or in other words, "to establish the accuracy or truth of."

As you study the roots in this chapter, think critically about how each word came to have the meaning it does.

Prefixes, roots, and suffixes are often called the building blocks of words. By combining your knowledge of prefixes, roots, and suffixes, you'll find that you can figure out many words by breaking them down into their parts. What parts make up the following words?

PREFIX	+	ROOT	+	SUFFIX	=	WORD
contra- (against)	+	*dict* (say or speak)	+	*-ion* (action, state, or condition)	=	contradiction (statement of the opposite)

One witness's <u>contradiction</u> of the other's testimony confused the jury.

ad- (to or near)	+	*here* (stick)	+	*-(e)nce* (state, quality, or process)	=	adherence (quality of sticking)

You'll get better <u>adherence</u> of the bumper sticker if you first clean the surface you're applying it to.

post- (after)	+	*pone* (put or place)	+	*-ment* (action, process, or result)	=	postponement (putting off until later)

Heavy rains caused the <u>postponement</u> of the game.

Words to Know: Vocabulary Lists and Activities

Greek and Latin have contributed thousands of words that have become part of the English language. In fact, the English language contains more words from Latin than from any other language. In this chapter, you will see many examples of words built on Greek and Latin roots.

Here are a few important points to remember.

> A root may have just one meaning (*bio* means "life," as in *biology* and *biographical*), or it may have more than one. For example, the Latin root *spect* may mean "see" or "look," as in *spectacle*, *spectator*, and *inspect*.

> Different roots can have the same meaning. For instance, the Latin root *script* and the Greek root *graph* both mean "write."

>> *script*: prescription, postscript

>> *graph*: graphic, seismograph

> Some roots are spelled in more than one way. For example, the root *pend* comes from Latin *pendere* and means "hang," as in *suspend* and *pendulum*. The same root is also spelled *pens*, as in *suspense* and *pensive*.

List 9 ## Words with Greek Roots

These four Greek roots make up a lot of words with which you're probably already familiar, especially academic words. Study the roots and ten words that are formed with them. Read each word, what it means, and how it's used.

Root	Meaning	Examples
chron, chrono	time	**chron**icle, **chrono**logical, syn**chron**ize
onym	name or word	an**onym**ous, ant**onym**, pseud**onym**
phil	love	**phil**anthropist, **phil**osophy
psych, psycho	mind	**psycho**logy, **psycho**sis

Word	What It Means	How It's Used
chronicle *(n)* KRAH-ni-kuhl	a historical account of events arranged in the order in which they occurred	The captain kept a detailed *chronicle* of the ship's travels.
chronological *(adj)* krah-nih-LAH-jih-kuhl	arranged in order of occurrence (The suffix *-ical* appears on List 7, page 39.)	The records in the file cabinet are arranged in *chronological* order.
synchronize *(v)* SING-kruh-nize	to cause to agree in time (The suffix *-ize* appears on List 6, page 34.)	The soldiers *synchronized* their watches before setting out on their mission.
anonymous *(adj)* uh-NAH-nuh-muhs	not named; unidentified (literally, "without name")	An *anonymous* donor made a generous contribution to our charity.
antonym *(n)* AN-tuh-nim	a word that means the opposite of another word	*High* and *low* are *antonyms.*
pseudonym *(n)* SOO-duh-nim	a false name	H. H. Munro writes stories under the *pseudonym* Saki.
philanthropist *(n)* fi-LAN-thruh-pist	someone who tries to promote human welfare, as by making charitable gifts	Thanks to the generosity of *philanthropists*, the food bank will be serving Thanksgiving dinner.

continued

philosophy *(n)* fi-LAH-suh-fee	the study of the basic principles and beliefs underlying human knowledge and behavior (from Greek *sophia*, "wisdom")	Students of *philosophy* search for the meaning of life.
psychology *(n)* sie-KAH-luh-jee	the scientific study of the mind and behavior	*Psychology* helps people understand human thought, feelings, and actions.
psychosis *(n)* sie-KOH-sis	a severe mental disorder	The patient had to be hospitalized for treatment of his *psychosis*.

Own It: Develop Your Word Understanding

Snip, Snip

Directions: In this activity, you'll use scissors to cut the root out of a vocabulary word. Why? To teach your classmates a thing or two. Follow these steps:

1. Your teacher will assign you a vocabulary word. Write your word in large block letters on a piece of paper. Set it aside.

2. Learn about your word. What does the word mean? What is the root? What is the root's meaning?

3. Grab a pair of scissors and the paper from step 1. It's showtime!

4. Stand in front of the class and hold up your word. Then do three things:

   a. Tell the class what the word means.

   b. Cut the root out of the word.

   c. Hold up the root and tell what the root means.

Note: You may not be the first student to teach your word to the class. If your word seems familiar to students, that's wonderful. It means that everyone is learning the vocabulary words. Your lesson will reinforce their knowledge.

Link It: Make Word-to-World Connections

Movie Poster

Directions: In this activity, you will create a movie poster that shows your knowledge of the vocabulary words. Follow these steps.

1. Gather materials to create a poster about a movie you like. You'll need poster board, magazine cutouts, photocopies, your own artwork, paints, pens, or similar supplies. (Alternative: If you can't think of a movie, you can create a poster about a book you've read.)

2. Plan your poster. Besides planning images, think about how you can incorporate a selection of vocabulary words. For example, you could make up one-line movie reviews, a statement telling about the plot, quotations from the actors, and so on.

3. Create the movie poster. Display your poster in class and point out the ways you used the vocabulary words to promote the movie.

Master It: Use Words in Meaningful Ways

Did You Know?

Directions: In this activity, you will choose one vocabulary word to explore further. Then you'll share a few facts with your classmates. Follow these steps:

1. Review the list of vocabulary words and their meanings. Choose one word that you find interesting.

2. Find *two or three* facts related to the word that you can share with your class. For instance, what is *synchronized* swimming? What are several methods of showing events in *chronological* order? Who are some authors that write/wrote using a *pseudonym*, and why did they do so? Useful sources of information include textbooks, nonfiction books, knowledgeable people, and articles.

3. Write a few sentences stating two or three facts related to the vocabulary word. Here are some phrases you could use to begin the sentences:

   > Did you know that . . .

   > Three things you need to know about (*vocabulary word*) are . . .

   > A question I had about (*vocabulary word*) was . . .

4. Practice reading your sentences aloud. Then read your sentences to your classmates.

List 10   Words with Latin Roots

The last list contained Greek roots; now study four Latin ones and words that are formed with them. Read each word, what it means, and how it's used.

Root	Meaning	Examples
dict	say; speak	e**dict**, ver**dict**
mit, miss	send	e**miss**ary, trans**mit**
tract	pull; move; draw	ab**stract**, de**tract**, re**tract**,
vers, vert	turn	a**vert**, contro**vers**y, di**vert**

Word	What It Means	How It's Used
edict (n) EE-dikt	an official public announcement having the force of law; decree	The king's *edict* banned certain forms of entertainment.
verdict (n) VUR-dikt	the decision of a judge or jury (literally, "true saying")	The jury reached a *verdict* of not guilty in the trial of the accused thief.
emissary (n) EH-muh-ser-ee	a person sent on a mission; representative	The government sent an *emissary* to participate in trade discussions.
transmit (v) trans-MIT	to pass on; convey	Certain mosquitoes can *transmit* malaria.
abstract (adj) ab-STRAKT	not representing an actual object or person	You need to use your imagination to appreciate *abstract* art.
detract (v) di-TRAKT	to reduce the quality or value of something	The abrupt ending *detracts* from an otherwise outstanding movie.
retract (v) ri-TRAKT	to draw back; take back	Once the cat felt relaxed, she *retracted* her claws.
avert (v) uh-VURT	to keep from happening; prevent; avoid (literally, "to turn away")	City officials believe that strengthening the dam will help to *avert* a disaster.
controversy (n) KON-truh-vur-see	dispute; disagreement	The dangerous experiment caused a *controversy* in the scientific community.
divert (v) di-VURT	to turn aside; redirect	Police *diverted* traffic away from the crash site.

> ### Tip
>
> The more word parts you learn, the more words you can add to your vocabulary and the better able you are to understand each word's meaning.
>
> Get into the habit of looking at words carefully and thinking about their parts. For example, in Chapter 2, you learned the suffixes *-able*, *-ical*, and *-ion*. In this chapter, you've learned the words *philosophy*, *psychology*, and *retract*. Using your knowledge of word parts, can you figure out the meaning of these words?
>
> psycholog<u>ical</u>   retract<u>ion</u>
>
> philosoph<u>ical</u>   retract<u>able</u>

Own It: Develop Your Word Understanding

Accept or Reject?

Directions: In this activity, you'll try to spot fake definitions of the vocabulary words. Here's how the activity works:

1. Your teacher will assign you and a partner one of the vocabulary words. On an index card, write your names and the word you received. On the back of the card, write a *correct* definition of the word and an *incorrect* definition that you make up. (Label each definition.) Make sure that your incorrect definition is still related to the correct one, so that the wrong answer is not too obvious.

2. Your teacher will mix everyone's cards together in a box.

3. Your teacher will pull out a card and read the vocabulary word aloud. Then he or she will read *one* of the definitions on the card.

4. Your teacher will ask for a show of hands to indicate whether you *accept* or *reject* the definition. Be prepared to defend your vote!

Once, I thought that if I got a short, spiky haircut, it would catch Emily's eye and <u>divert</u> her attention away from the hockey player she'd been talking to. So I went to the barber, but as soon as he started chopping, I wished I could <u>retract</u> my decision... I'm glad my hair has grown back out!

Link It: Make Word-to-World Connections

Where in the World?

Directions: Where in *your* world would you most likely encounter the things, ideas, and actions named by the vocabulary words? With a partner, discuss how you might encounter each one. Then write each word in one of the boxes below. *Bonus:* Add your own heading to the empty box and add words to this box too. (You may write a word in more than one box.)

In a class discussion, explain your categorization of the words.

at home	in a class
out having fun	

Master It: Use Words in Meaningful Ways

Transmit Your Knowledge

Directions: In the previous activity, you sorted vocabulary words based on where in the world you would most likely find them. Now use one vocabulary word as a doorway into that world. How? By writing a fictional or factual piece inspired by the key word. Here are a few ideas:

> a short story about a *controversy* in a family

> an article about the Edict of Milan, the Edict of Worms, or another *edict* in history

> an explanation of *abstract* art for those new to the subject

Before you begin, ask your teacher to approve your topic. Then research (if necessary) and write the fictional or factual piece. Aim for a length of *1 to 2 pages*. Your teacher will collect everyone's papers in a folder. When you have spare time in class, indulge your curiosity by pulling out someone else's work and reading it.

More About Words from Greek

If you look back at the word lists you've studied, you may notice an interesting difference between words that come from Greek and words that come from Latin. Words from Latin generally combine one root with a prefix, suffix, or both. Words from Greek, however, often (but not always) combine two roots. Compare these examples:

LATIN PREFX + ROOT	LATIN ROOT + SUFFIX	GREEK ROOT + ROOT
contradict	amorous	philosophy
extract	fortify	pseudonym
postpone	invincible	psychology

Greek roots are also interesting in that so many of the nouns can be changed to adjectives by adding the suffix *-ic* or *-ical* (see List 7, page 39) and to adverbs by adding the suffix *-ly* (see List 8, page 45). Look at these examples:

NOUN	ADJECTIVE	ADVERB
(Greek root)	(adds *-ic* or *-ical*)	(adds *-ly*)
chronology	chronological	chronologically
ecology	ecologic or ecological	ecologically
mythology	mythological	mythologically
philosophy	philosophical or philosophic	philosophically
psychology	psychological	psychologically

Wrapping Up: Review What You've Learned

Here's a brief summary of what you've studied in this chapter.

> A **root** is a word part from which other words are formed. A root differs from a base word. A base word can stand alone, while a root usually cannot.

> Like prefixes and suffixes, roots also come from other languages, such as Greek and Latin.

> A root may have just one meaning, or it may have more than one.

> Different roots can have the same meaning.

> Some roots are spelled in more than one way.

> Roots may appear at the beginning, in the middle, or at the end of a word.

> While a root by itself may not look familiar, learning its meaning will give you an important clue to the meaning of every word built on that root. Some roots will help you understand large families of words.

> Words from Latin generally combine one root with a prefix, suffix, or both. Words that come from Greek often (but not always) combine two roots.

> Many nouns with Greek roots can be changed to adjectives by adding the suffix *-ic* or *-ical* and to adverbs by adding the suffix *-ly*.

> You have learned the following Greek and Latin roots and words made from them. Can you recall what these roots mean? Page numbers are listed so that you can check your answer if you're not sure.

chron, chrono (**page 59**)	dict (**page 62**)
onym (**page 59**)	mit, miss (**page 62**)
phil (**page 59**)	tract (**page 62**)
psych, psycho (**page 59**)	vers, vert (**page 62**)

Flaunt It: Show Your Word Understanding

In the following exercises, you'll demonstrate your understanding of each vocabulary word. You will use vocabulary words, or forms of the words, to complete sentences and to write sentences of your own.

A **Word Bank**

Directions: Write words from the box to complete each sentence. You will not use all of the words.

abstract	edict	psychosis
anonymous	emissary	retract
antonym	philanthropist	synchronize
avert	philosophy	transmit
controversy	pseudonym	verdict
divert	psychology	

1. Jasmine's uncle is a _____, but he prefers to remain _____ when he donates large sums to worthy causes.

2. While studying _____, Dr. Boone became an expert on body language, which can _____ information without the use of words.

3. To _____ an argument, Eric tried to _____ his brother's attention away from the ruined music player.

4. The defendant's _____ had a direct influence on the jury's _____ in her case.

5. My new "friend" turned out to be a/an _____ from an awful group of girls who like to stir up _____ in other students' lives.

B **Sentence Completion**

Directions: Circle the letter of the word that best completes each sentence.

6. Ryan asked a librarian to recommend a/an _____ of pioneer life, written from the point of view of a teenager.

    a. chronicle
    b. verdict
    c. pseudonym
    d. edict

7. "Please write an essay that explains your _____ of friendship," Mrs. Dietz said.

   a. philanthropist   **b.** abstract
   c. psychosis   **d.** philosophy

8. A/an _____ at some schools is the question of whether to require students to wear uniforms.

   a. psychology   **b.** controversy
   c. emissary   **d.** antonym

9. In a story, a flashback interrupts the _____ order of events.

   a. synchronize   **b.** anonymous
   c. transmit   **d.** chronological

10. Please _____ your eyes while I dial the combination to the safe.

   a. divert   **b.** detract
   c. avert   **d.** retract

(Writing

Directions: Write one or more sentences to answer each question. In your response, use the italicized key word, or a form of it. Write your sentences on a separate sheet of paper.

11. What is your *philosophy* on revenge?

12. How can you help a friend put an *abstract* idea into words?

13. What is something a friend does that *detracts* from your friendship?

14. What is an *edict* that governs your behavior?

15. What author used the *pseudonym* Mark Twain?

16. In a *chronicle* of your school year, what would be the first event?

17. When was the last time you said something that you wish you could *retract*?

18. What are your three favorite memories, listed in *chronological* order?

19. What is an *antonym* of the word *rapid*?

20. When a singer lip-synchs, or *synchronizes*, a song, what is he or she doing?

Activities à la Carte: Extend Your Word Knowledge

The activities on this page are presented à la carte, like items on a restaurant menu, meaning that you can choose from a variety of options. Your teacher may assign an activity or let you pick the one that tempts your appetite. If time allows, you might do more than one activity. All of the activities feature the same ingredient: **roots**. Dig in!

Family Reunion

Choose a Greek or Latin root and create a poster showing a family of words that use this root. On the poster, include a definition of the root's meaning and list as many words as you can discover that use this root. Colorful paints or artwork will make the poster eye-catching. Display your creation in class.

Your Roots Are Showing

Have you ever had a *root* canal? Have you eaten a *root* vegetable? Have you traced your family's *roots*? These are just a few of the many uses of *root*, a multiple-meaning word. Make a poster or computer presentation to teach your classmates different uses of *root*. Be sure to use visuals, along with words, to get your ideas across.

Tinker with It

Tinker with the vocabulary words in this chapter, changing them into other parts of speech. You'll notice that the same root is evident in each word form. For instance, *psychology* becomes *psychologist* and *psychological*. Share some of the results with your class. Discuss how this knowledge of roots and word forms could come in handy.

Movie Pitch

Use vocabulary words in this chapter to inspire ideas for a movie. Alone or with a partner, write a plot summary to tell what your movie is about. Write a list of characters with brief descriptions of each. Finally, pitch your movie idea to the class. Ask for a show of hands indicating who would go see your movie.

Digging up Roots

You studied some roots in this chapter, but where can you find additional roots, meanings, and examples? Do a survey of sources available, such as Web sites and study aids. Create a list of sources and write notes about the information available from each source. Post your list in class, or pass out copies to classmates.

 ## Compare and Contrast

Find out if a word with a Greek or Latin root in English has the same root if translated into another language. But don't stop there—translate the word into three different languages. You can use an online translation tool, or use translation dictionaries in a library. Create a table showing the results and draw some conclusions from these results. Share your findings with others who enjoy languages and translation.

A Page from Your Future

Create a book called *Pages from My Future*. Devote each page of the book to a different vocabulary word and relate the word to a profession or activity. What would you do as a *philanthropist*? Do you see yourself teaching *psychology* or becoming a political or religious *emissary*? Illustrate each page with a drawing, photo, or other image.

Forming Words with Prefixes and Suffixes

4

D o you have an old box of Legos stashed in your room at home? Or a few jigsaw puzzles, a bead jewelry kit, or a model race car kit? Like most people, you probably have experience putting together parts to create a whole. You know that the success of the final product depends on the parts that make it up. You can create different results by combining the parts in various ways.

Words are no different. You have studied the basic parts of words: prefixes, suffixes, and base words and roots. In this chapter, you'll take a closer look at how all of these parts can be combined—and *re*combined.

Objectives

In this chapter, you will learn

> How to add prefixes and suffixes to form new words

> Common words with multiple word parts (prefixes *and* suffixes)

Sneak Peek: Preview the Lesson

Skim and Scan

As you may know, you can determine what a chapter is about by skimming and scanning it. To **skim** a chapter, you run your eyes over the headings, tables, and other features to get an idea of what the chapter is about. To **scan** a chapter, you run your eyes over headings and paragraphs, looking for particular words or ideas. Skimming and scanning allow you to get useful information quickly.

1. What can you find out by skimming this chapter? **Skim** the headings, tables, and any other features that stand out. Then write a few phrases or sentences identifying what topics you think the chapter will cover.

_____

_____

_____

2. Scan the chapter for key words such as _prefix, suffix, root,_ and _base._ Besides these, what other key words stand out? Based on your scan, what do you expect the chapter to teach you?

_____

_____

_____

Vocabulary Mini-Lesson: How to Add Prefixes and Suffixes

As a general rule, it's easy to add a prefix to a word. Don't let spelling confuse you. Just keep all the letters of both the prefix and the base word.

Study the following examples, which use some of the prefixes you learned in Chapter 1. Notice that no letters are left out or changed, even when the last letter of the prefix is the same as the first letter of the base word.

PREFIX	+	BASE WORD	=	NEW WORD
anti	+	war	=	antiwar
im	+	mature	=	immature
in	+	convenient	=	inconvenient
ir	+	responsible	=	irresponsible
post	+	date	=	postdate
semi	+	annual	=	semiannual
super	+	human	=	superhuman

It's a little bit trickier to attach a suffix to a word than it is to add a prefix. Most of the time, you'll keep all the letters of both the suffix and the word and not drop, change, or add any letters. In forming the following words, there are no letters dropped or omitted.

BASE WORD	+	SUFFIX	=	NEW WORD
digest	+	-ible	=	digestible
exist	+	-ence	=	existence
hero	+	-ic	=	heroic
less	+	-en	=	lessen

partner	+	-ship	=	partnership
patriot	+	-ism	=	patriotism
popular	+	-ize	=	popularize
prevent	+	-ive	=	preventive
relax	+	-ation	=	relaxation
resist	+	-ance	=	resistance
rhythm	+	-ical	=	rhythmical
triumphant	+	-ly	=	triumphantly
vigor	+	-ous	=	vigorous

However, sometimes adding a suffix *does* affect the spelling of a word. This usually happens when you add suffixes to words ending in *y*, and when you add suffixes to words ending in silent *e*. Let's look at both of these cases, using suffixes that you learned in Chapter 2.

Adding Suffixes to Words That End in *Y*

When it comes to attaching suffixes, words ending in *y* can cause some confusion. That's because not all *y*-ending words follow the same rule. The key is to look at the letter *before* the *y*.

> If the letter before the *y* is a *consonant*, change the *y* to *i* before adding the suffix.

BASE WORD	+	SUFFIX	=	NEW WORD
angry	+	-ly	=	angrily
defy	+	-ant	=	defiant
economy	+	-ical	=	economical
envy	+	-able	=	enviable
fantasy	+	-ize	=	fantasize
mystery	+	-ous	=	mysterious
psychology	+	-ical	=	psychological
strategy	+	-ic	=	strategic

Note: There are a few exceptions to this rule, such as *shyness* and *shyly*, *dryness*, *slyness* and *slyly*, and *wryness* and *wryly*.

> If the letter before the *y* is a *vowel*, do *not* change the *y* to *i* before adding the suffix.

BASE WORD	+	SUFFIX	=	NEW WORD
betray	+	-al	=	betrayal
coy	+	-ly	=	coyly
joy	+	-ous	=	joyous
key	+	-less	=	keyless
survey	+	-or	=	surveyor
way	+	-ward	=	wayward

Note: One exception to this rule is *daily*.

Adding Suffixes to Words That End with a Silent *E*

Many words end in a silent *e*. This means that the *e* is not pronounced, as in *plate* and *survive*. There are two general rules for attaching suffixes to words ending with a silent *e*. The key is to look at the first letter of the suffix.

> If the suffix starts with a *vowel*, drop the silent *e*.

BASE WORD	+	SUFFIX	=	NEW WORD
active	+	-ate	=	activate
adventure	+	-ous	=	adventurous
defense	+	-ive	=	defensive
resemble	+	-ance	=	resemblance
reverse	+	-ible	=	reversible
starve	+	-ation	=	starvation

Note: There are some exceptions to this rule. Words ending in *ge*, such as *courageous* and *outrageous*, keep the silent *e*. In addition, words ending in *able* sometimes keep the silent *e*. Examples: *agreeable, knowledgeable, changeable, manageable, noticeable,* and *rechargeable.* Other *able* words do follow the rule and drop the silent *e*: *believable, desirable, usable, lovable, excusable.*

> If the suffix starts with a *consonant*, keep the silent *e*.

BASE WORD	+	SUFFIX	=	NEW WORD
amuse	+	-ment	=	amusement
false	+	-ly	=	falsely
grace	+	-ful	=	graceful
home	+	-ward	=	homeward
like	+	-wise	=	likewise
safe	+	-ty	=	safety
same	+	-ness	=	sameness

Note: Exceptions to this rule include *judgment, argument,* and *truly.*

> However, when you change an adjective ending in -*le* to an adverb ending in -*ly*, you drop the silent *e*.

ADJECTIVE	+	SUFFIX	=	ADVERB
comfortable	+	-ly	=	comfortably
illegible	+	-ly	=	illegibly
probable	+	-ly	=	probably
responsible	+	-ly	=	responsibly
terrible	+	-ly	=	terribly

Words to Know: Vocabulary Lists and Activities

Many words contain two or more prefixes or suffixes. Your knowledge of word parts can help you figure out the meaning of such words. Study the following lists. The letters in dark type are prefixes and suffixes that you learned in Chapters 1 and 2. You may recognize some other word parts as well.

List 11   Words with Multiple Parts

Read each word, what it means, and how it's used.

Word	What It Means	How It's Used
adapt**ation** *(n)* a-dap-TAY-shuhn	a composition rewritten or otherwise changed to make it suitable for a new use	The movie *To Kill a Mockingbird* is an *adaptation* of the well-known novel.
addict**ive** *(adj)* uh-DIK-tiv	causing addiction (You studied the root *dict* in Chapter 3, page 62.)	Sleeping pills can become *addictive* if used for too long.
adher**ence** *(n)* ad-HERE-uhns	obedience; observance	Membership in our club requires strict *adherence* to the rules.
admir**able** *(adj)* AD-mer-uh-buhl	deserving to be admired or praised	Michael's study habits are *admirable*.
admitt**ance** *(n)* ad-MIH-tunts	permission to enter (You studied the root *mit* in Chapter 3, page 62.)	*Admittance* to the special museum exhibit is restricted to adults.
advers**ely** *(adv)* ad-VURS-lee	in a harmful way; unfavorably; negatively (You studied the root *vers* in Chapter 3, page 62.)	The pollution caused by motor vehicles *adversely* affects our environment.
emerg**ence** *(n)* i-MUR-juhnts	process or fact of becoming known	Bears' *emergence* from hibernation occurs when winter is over.
eros**ive** *(adj)* i-ROH-siv	causing erosion; wearing away	The *erosive* effects of wind and water have damaged the shoreline.

continued

| evasion *(n)*
 i-VAY-zhuhn | act of avoiding something; avoidance | Reporters accused the governor of *evasion* because he would not answer their questions. |
| exclusive *(adj)*
 iks-KLOO-siv | limited to certain people only | Only invited celebrities were admitted to the *exclusive* Hollywood party. |

Own It: Develop Your Word Understanding

Exploring Key Words

Directions: Work with a partner to complete the activity. Each of you should complete five of the graphic organizers. Then share your results. For each graphic organizer, follow these steps:

1. Study the vocabulary word and its definition in List 11. Then use your own words and ideas to write a definition in the center box, labeled "my definition."

2. In the left-hand box, divide the word into syllables. Try this on your own; then check your work with a dictionary.

3. Finally, play around with the word's parts. Add and remove prefixes and suffixes to create other forms of the word. (For instance, *addictive* is an adjective form of the noun *addiction*. You can change *adversely* to *conversely* by changing prefixes.) Write these words in the right-hand box. Check your answers with your teacher or in a dictionary.

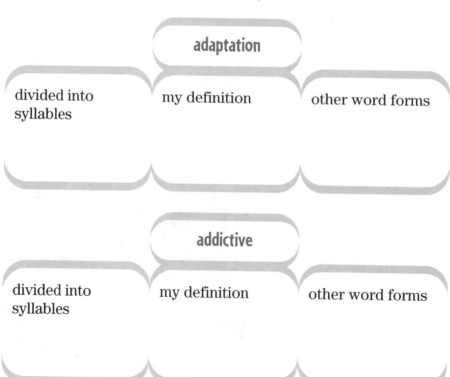

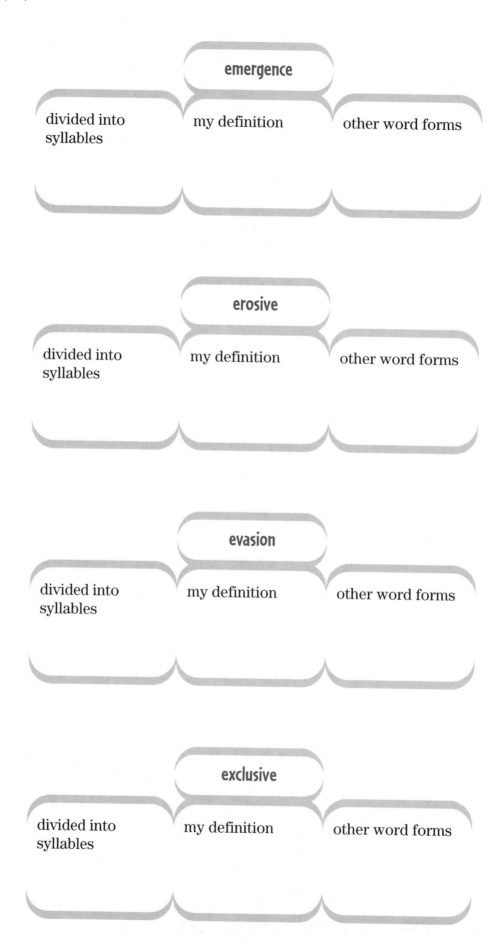

emergence

divided into syllables

my definition

other word forms

erosive

divided into syllables

my definition

other word forms

evasion

divided into syllables

my definition

other word forms

exclusive

divided into syllables

my definition

other word forms

Normally, I <u>adhere</u> to a pretty healthy diet, but I find chocolate chip cookies to be <u>addictive</u>. If I eat too many before a soccer game, though, I get a stomachache that <u>adversely</u> affects my playing.

Link It: Make Word-to-World Connections

Me, Myself, and I

Directions: Follow these steps to complete the activity. Your teacher may ask you to work with a partner.

1. Think about how the key word—or another form of the word—relates to you. For instance, can you use the word in a description of yourself? In a comment about a friend? In a description of a dream or favorite activity? In a statement about your community?

2. In the space beside each key word, write a sentence or two telling what the word has to do with you and your world. Be sure to use the key word in your response!

Key Word	What This Word Has to Do with Me
adaptation	
addictive	
adherence	
admirable	

continued

admittance	
adversely	
emergence	
erosive	
evasion	
exclusive	

Master It: Use Words in Meaningful Ways

Word Problems

Directions: In a class or small group discussion, answer each of the following questions. Explain your reasoning.

1. Is it ever *admirable* to use *addictive* substances?
2. When does *evasion* of responsibility lead to *erosive* effects on the environment?
3. Should an *adaptation* show perfect *adherence* to the original?
4. How might an *exclusive* party affect someone *adversely*?
5. How might *admittance* to a class lead to the *emergence* of a passion?

List 12 Words with Multiple Parts

Read each word, what it means, and how it's used.

Word	What It Means	How It's Used
expiration *(n)* ek-spuh-RAY-shuhn	coming to an end; termination	I have to renew my library card before its *expiration* in June.
exposition *(n)* ek-spuh-ZIH-shun	writing or speech that is meant to give information or explain something	Our teacher asked us to write an *exposition* on why music and art classes are beneficial to a person's education.

continued

impuls**ively** *(adv)* im-PUHL-siv-lee	quickly and with little or no forethought	Charlotte *impulsively* chose the garlic broccoli from the menu and later regretted it.
incap**able** *(adj)* in-KAY-puh-buhl	(used with *of*) not having the ability	Young children seem *incapable* of sitting still.
indispens**able** *(adj)* in-di-SPEN-suh-buhl	absolutely necessary; essential	Power tools are *indispensable* to a carpenter.
inflex**ible** *(adj)* in-FLEK-suh-buhl	not open to change or compromise; rigid; unyielding	Mr. Hakim is an *inflexible* man who won't change his mind once he's made a decision.
intang**ible** *(adj)* in-TAN-juh-buhl	not capable of being touched; not easily defined or grasped	Thomas has an *intangible* quality that makes him a natural leader.
irrevers**ible** *(adj)* ir-i-VUHR-suh-buhl	not able to be reversed or changed back	The actress made an *irreversible* decision to turn down the lead role in that movie.
monoton**ously** *(adv)* muh-NAH-teh-nuhs-lee	with little or no variation; in a boring or tedious way	Mrs. Palisano's lecture seemed endless, her words droning on *monotonously* as listeners fought to stay awake.
supervis**ion** *(n)* soo-per-VIH-zhuhn	overseeing; direction	Children are not allowed in the swimming pool without adult *supervision*.

Own It: Develop Your Word Understanding

Break It Up!

Directions: Your teacher will divide the class into ten small groups. Each group will be assigned one vocabulary word. In your group, follow these steps:

1. Break the word into its parts. You'll have a base word or root plus one or more prefixes and suffixes. Write each word part on an index card.

2. Look up the meanings of prefixes and suffixes in Chapters 1 and 2 of this book. Write the meanings of these word parts on the backs of the cards.

3. Read your vocabulary word aloud to the class. Identify the prefix(es) and suffix(es), and state their meanings. Then tell how these "affixes" work with the base words or roots to form the complete vocabulary word.

Link It: Make Word-to-World Connections

Have You Ever . . .

Directions: Your teacher will get the activity started by asking a student one of the questions in the box. That person answers by saying yes or no and gives an explanation. Then that person asks someone else a question.

You can use one of the questions that follow or make up your own question using a vocabulary word.

Have you ever . . .

. . . eaten or drunk something after its *expiration* date?

. . . acted *impulsively*?

. . . felt *incapable* of doing something—and then you did it anyway?

. . . been *indispensable* to another person (for a project, activity, etc.)?

. . . felt frustrated when someone else was *inflexible*?

. . . admired an *intangible* quality in a friend?

. . . regretted making an *irreversible* decision?

. . . written an *exposition* on animal rights?

. . . felt disappointed when a party/event went on *monotonously*?

. . . wished you had less adult *supervision*?

Master It: Use Words in Meaningful Ways

Blog

Directions: Use a vocabulary word to inspire a blog entry. For ideas, you could think about experiences that people described in the Have You Ever . . . activity above. Or you could use a vocabulary word to create an entirely original blog entry to express yourself, entertain readers, ponder a problem, or achieve some other purpose. Write at least three paragraphs. Happy blogging!

Wrapping Up: Review What You've Learned

Here's a brief summary of what you've studied in this chapter.

> In general, to add a prefix to a base word, keep all the letters of both the prefix and the word, even when the last letter of the prefix is the same as the first letter of the word.

> Most of the time, to attach a suffix, keep all the letters of both the suffix and the word and do not drop, change, or add any letters. However, sometimes special rules apply.

> To add a suffix to a word that ends in *y*, look at the letter before the *y*. If the letter before the *y* is a consonant, change the *y* to *i* before adding the suffix. If the letter before the *y* is a vowel, do *not* change the *y* to *i* before adding the suffix.

> To add a suffix to a word that ends in a silent *e*, look at the first letter of the suffix. If the suffix starts with a vowel, drop the silent *e* before adding the suffix. If the suffix starts with a consonant, keep the silent *e*. (But: When changing an adjective ending in -*le* to an adverb ending in -*ly*, drop the silent *e*.)

Chapter Review Exercises

Flaunt It: Show Your Word Understanding

In the following exercises, you'll demonstrate your understanding of each vocabulary word. You will use vocabulary words, or forms of the words, to complete sentences and to write sentences of your own.

A Word Bank

Directions: Write words from the box to complete the story.

> adaptation   admirably   admittance   indispensable
> addictive   impulsively   monotonously

I was so excited when I received a letter of **(1)**_____ from drama camp!

Before we could act in a play, we learned some do's and don'ts. It is important to speak with enthusiasm, not **(2)**_____. Also, we were warned not to speak **(3)**_____ and interrupt but to wait for our turn.

Together, we wrote a stage **(4)**_____ of "All Summer in a Day" by Ray Bradbury. I played Margot, the girl who gets locked in the closet. The audience said I performed **(5)**_____ and was a/an **(6)**_____ member of the cast.

Being onstage is **(7)**_____! I want to have a career in acting.

B Sentence Completion

Directions: Circle the letter of the word that best completes each sentence.

8. Aaron failed to make the track team because he is _____ of running a quarter mile without stopping.

    a. irreversible   **b.** incapable
    c. intangible   **d.** indispensable

9. After his novel was praised by critics, the author sold _____ rights to the book to a major film company.

    a. erosive   **b.** admirable
    c. exclusive   **d.** evasive

10. For _____ to the boarding area, you must show a plane ticket and pass through a security check.

   a. admittance   **b.** emergence
   c. supervision   **d.** adaptation

11. Do you believe that drinking sugary beverages is _____ or that it is non-habit-forming?

   a. monotonous   **b.** adverse
   c. impulsive   **d.** addictive

12. My chief complaint is that you always try to _____ my time and attention.

   a. adhere   **b.** inflexible
   c. expire   **d.** monopolize

(Writing

Directions: Write one or more sentences to answer each question. In your response, use the italicized key word or a form of it. Write your sentences on a separate sheet of paper.

13. What is one thing that you are *incapable* of doing?

14. What is one rule of thumb to which you *adhere*?

15. How might someone be affected *adversely* by telling the truth?

16. When did you notice the *emergence* of a new skill in a friend?

17. What is one of your *intangible* qualities?

18. When was a time when you made an *irreversible* decision?

19. Where might you see a sign that says, "Adult *supervision* required"?

20. What part of your weekly schedule is *inflexible*?

Chapter Extension Activities

Activities à la Carte: Extend Your Word Knowledge

The activities on this page are presented à la carte, like items on a restaurant menu, meaning that you can choose from a variety of options. Your teacher may assign an activity or let you pick the one that tempts your appetite. If time allows, you might do more than one activity. All of the activities feature the same ingredient: **word parts**. Dig in!

Fakability Test

Use word parts from Chapters 1–4 of this book to create real-sounding **fake** words. A few examples to get you started are *adversement*, *flexify*, and *impulsible*. Make up a stack of index cards, writing a real or a fake word on each. Test friends and friendly adults to see who can sort real from fake.

Disc Jockey

If you love music *and* love to talk, you may be a DJ at heart. To give this enterprise a whirl, host a party where you'll be the DJ. Plan the music to fit the party's theme, mood, or purpose. Then write snippets of chatter to read between song sets. Use some of the vocabulary words to inspire topics and ideas. Finally, party, party, party!

You Crack Me Up

Dust off your funny bone and grab a pencil. Create a single-frame cartoon using a vocabulary word (or form of a word) from this chapter. For instance, how would you illustrate the phrase, "When *supervision* requires super vision" or the sentence "Roger discovered that jelly beans were *indispensable*"?

Top Ten

Make a list of your top ten favorite books or music albums or movies. Then analyze the titles. What prefixes and suffixes do you recognize? What roots and base words are familiar to you? Are these titles formed mostly of multipart words or simpler words? Share your findings with your class.

The Write Stuff

Compete with friends to see who can use word parts in this chapter to create the most new words in five minutes. Open your book to the two word lists (pages 75 and 80). Then set a timer for five minutes. Create new words and word forms by taking roots and adding different prefixes and suffixes. Then give your new words a reality check—are they real words? Ask your teacher if you can post your list on a class bulletin board.

ELL ¡Que Misterioso!

Translate each word in this chapter's word lists into a second language. Is there a direct translation for each word, or must you use a phrase? Can you break the translated word into the same parts as those in the English word? Would you say that one language relies on prefixes and suffixes more than the other language, or do they use these word parts about equally? Share your findings with someone who's interested in languages.

One for the Money

Earn money by marketing your services as a babysitter, dog walker, yard cleaner, or all-purpose helper. Using new words you've learned, create a flyer. On it, hook clients with a witty sentence such as, "Enjoy life's *intangible* pleasures, and leave the dishes to me" or "Having me wash your car twice a month is *addictive*!" Include your pay rate and contact information, and distribute flyers to people you know.

Rooted in You

Get together with a friend and entertain each other with some wordplay. Using each other's name as a root, add prefixes or suffixes to invent new words. Create a definition to go with each new word. For instance, what does it mean to *Mikeify* something? What does *injordanable* mean? Share your favorite new word with the class.

Learning Words from Other Sources

5

D o you know what a *dead* language is?
Or what a *living* language is?
A dead language is no longer learned as the native language of a people. Take Latin, for instance. It exists as a language, but is it not the native language of any country or people. Dead languages are frozen in time. No new words are being added to reflect changing times.

In contrast, a living language is one that is currently learned as a native language. As people learn and use the language, they bring changes to it. They may incorporate foreign words, for example, or create new words.

In this chapter, you'll study English as a living language. You'll learn a range of words from different sources that have been added to English.

Objectives

In this chapter, you will learn

> How new words come into our language from foreign languages, from mythology, and from the names of people, places, or things

> Common words from some of these various sources

Sneak Peek: Preview the Lesson

Beg, Borrow, or Steal

The following table lists a few sources of words added to the English language. To become familiar with each type of source, respond to the questions in the second column. *Hint:* Consult a reference source for help with unfamiliar terms.

Some Sources of Words	Questions for Thought
foreign languages	What are the names of a few foreign languages? Do you ever use a word from one of these languages when you're speaking in English? Explain.
mythology	What are myths? Can you name any characters from myths?
proper nouns	What are proper nouns? Can you think of any words formed from proper nouns?

Vocabulary Mini-Lesson: Words Come from Foreign Languages

What do the following words have in common?

algebra	apricot	giraffe	jar
mattress	sherbet	sofa	zero

All of these words have been adopted into English from Arabic.

Words from foreign languages have been added to English over hundreds of years, and they are still being added today. Over the centuries, whenever English speakers came into contact with people from other cultures through trade, travel, or war, they adopted or "borrowed" some of their words. These words may not seem foreign to us, either because their form and spelling have changed or simply because we are so used to hearing them. For example, *canyon* and *mosquito* are words of Spanish origin, while *piano* and *confetti* come from Italian. You may be surprised at the origin of some of the words in the following lists.

 ords to Know: Vocabulary Lists and Activities

In this section, you'll study two lists of words from foreign languages.

List 13   Words from Foreign Languages

Here are common words from French, Spanish, Italian, and Hindi. Read each word, its source, what it means, and how it's used.

Word	Its Source	What It Means	How It's Used
bizarre *(adj)* bi-ZAHR	French	strikingly odd or unusual; strange	The circus clown wore a *bizarre* combination of bright purple pants and an orange-striped coat.
bodega *(n)* boh-DAY-guh	Spanish	a small grocery store	Maria purchased fresh vegetables at the *bodega*.
boutique *(n)* boo-TEEK	French	a small shop that sells fashionable, generally expensive, items	The dress in the *boutique* window was beautiful, but I couldn't afford to buy it.
cliché *(n)* klee-SHAY	French	an expression or idea that has been worn out by too much use	"Don't put off until tomorrow what you can do today" has become a *cliché*.
connoisseur *(n)* kah-nuh-SUR	French	someone who is an expert in a particular area, such as art or food	Mr. Rimbaud is a *connoisseur* of Impressionist painting.
coup d'état *(n)* koo-day-TAH	French	the sudden, violent overthrow of a ruler or government by a small group of people (literally, "stroke of state")	A 1973 *coup d'état* in Chile toppled the government and brought to power the brutal dictator Augusto Pinochet.
dinghy *(n)* DING-gee	Hindi	a small boat	Passengers used a *dinghy* to come ashore from the anchored ship.
encore *(n)* ON-kawr	French	a demand by the audience for another appearance of a performer; the appearance in response to such a demand (literally, "again")	The people stood and cheered, their nonstop applause calling the singer back for another *encore*.

continued

envoy *(n)* EN-voy	French	a person sent to represent one government in dealing with another; representative	Spain sent an *envoy* to France to negotiate a trade agreement.
fiasco *(n)* fee-AS-koh	Italian	a complete failure	Although she was a successful novelist, the author's attempt to write poetry was a *fiasco*.

Did You Know?

Words often trace their origin through two or more languages. For example, the word *czar* came to English from Russian but derives from Latin *Caesar*. *Adobe* had its origin in Egyptian, then passed into Arabic, and then into Spanish on its way into English.

Own It: Develop Your Word Understanding

Sensory Appeal

Directions: Study the list of vocabulary words and their meanings. Then take a moment to let each word come alive in your imagination. How? Think about how each word might appeal to one of the five senses. For instance, *boutique* may appeal to your sense of smell as you imagine expensive French perfumes sold in a boutique. *Encore* may appeal to your sense of hearing as you imagine a singer being called back onstage for an encore.

Write each vocabulary word and a brief description of its appeal to you in one of the boxes that follow. You may choose to record a word in more than one box.

Sense	How Each Vocabulary Word Appeals to That Sense
sight	
hearing	
taste	
touch	
smell	

Link It: Make Word-to-World Connections

Now and Later

Directions: In this activity, you'll think about words you're learning now and how these words may come in handy later. Pair up with a classmate and follow these steps:

1. One of you reads the first vocabulary word aloud. Together, make sure that you understand the meaning of the word.

2. On a sheet of paper, write the word. Then write an example of when or how you might use this word in the future.

3. Repeat steps 1 and 2 for each word in the list.

4. In a class discussion, share some of your results. Point out any words you don't see yourself using —and be surprised and informed by how others *do* plan to use the words!

I buy candy from the local <u>bodega</u> next to school, but my mom—a <u>connoisseur</u> of fancy French chocolates—prefers to buy candy from an expensive <u>boutique</u> downtown. Me, I can't taste the difference. I just need sugar!

Master It: Use Words in Meaningful Ways

Pick Three

Directions: In this activity, you'll help classmates become familiar with three vocabulary words that you know something about. Follow these steps:

1. Pick three vocabulary words that are familiar or interesting to you. (For ideas, review the two activities previous to this one.)

2. Write two or three sentences about each of the three words. Do your best to make the meaning of the word clear in the context of what you write. For instance, you could give specific examples of *clichés* or describe some *fiascoes* you've been involved in.

3. Your teacher will pronounce each vocabulary word aloud. After saying each word, he or she will ask students to read sentences that tell about that word.

List 14   Words from Foreign Languages

The following list contains common words from French, Spanish, Malay, Dutch, Hindi, and Latin. Read each word, its source, what it means, and how it's used.

Word	Its Source	What It Means	How It's Used
forte *(n)* FOR-tay	French	something a person does especially well; strong point	Ethan wants to join the debating team because public speaking is his *forte*.
genre *(n)* ZHAHN-ruh	French	a kind or type of literature, art, or music	The author has written many plays, but fiction remains the *genre* for which she is best known.
guerrilla *(n)* guh-RIH-luh	Spanish	member of a force of soldiers not part of a regular military unit, who harass the enemy and cause destruction	Government soldiers combed the jungle in search of the *guerrillas* who had blown up the bridge.
nonchalant *(adj)* non-shuh-LAHNT	French	seeming to be indifferent; unconcerned	Kim pretended to be *nonchalant* as she opened the envelope, but her heart was pounding.
orangutan *(n)* uh-RANG-uh-tan	Malay	a large ape found in Borneo and Sumatra (literally, "man of the forest")	The *orangutan* we saw at the zoo had very long arms and reddish-brown hair.
regime *(n)* ruh-ZHEEM	French	a government in power	The people's demands for free elections threatened to bring down the present *regime*.
silo *(n)* SIE-loh	Spanish	a pit or cylindrical building in which food for livestock is stored	The farmer feeds his cattle and horses with food from the *silo*.
sloop *(n)* sloop	Dutch	a sailboat with a single mast	The vacationers plan to sail their *sloop* to the Bahamas.
veranda *(n)* vuh-RAN-duh	Hindi	an open porch, usually roofed, along one or more sides of a building	We sat out on the *veranda*, sipping iced tea and enjoying the view.
vice versa *(adv)* VIE-suh VUR-suh	Latin	the order or relation reversed; the other way around	Sarah does not like dogs, and *vice versa*.

Did You Know?

Just as English has borrowed from other languages, so have other languages borrowed from English. In fact, English words appear in most languages of the world, in either their original or a changed form. Japanese, for example, has its own version of such common English words as *leader* (*lihda*) and *computer* (*konpyuta*), while France has borrowed *drugstore* and Spain has borrowed *e-mail*.

Own It: Develop Your Word Understanding

Think Fast

Directions: In this activity, you'll mingle with classmates—two minutes at a time! Here's what to do:

1. Your teacher will assign you a vocabulary word. Write it at the top of a sheet of paper. Then grab a pencil, stand up, and get ready to mingle.

2. Your teacher will announce, "Start." You have one minute to pair up with a classmate and, together, write a logical sentence using both of your vocabulary words.

3. After one minute, your teacher will call time. Quickly, write down the sentence you composed (if you haven't already). If the sentence seems illogical, or you were unable to write a sentence, make a note of that.

4. Then get ready to go again and pair up with someone different.

5. When the activity is over, read one of your sentences aloud to the class.

Link It: Make Word-to-World Connections

Q and A

Directions: In this activity, you'll use vocabulary words in questions for an interviewee of your choice. Follow these steps:

1. Skim the list of vocabulary words and their meanings. Think about people you know who seem linked to a few of the words. Choose one of these people to interview.

2. With this person in mind, write five interview questions. Use a vocabulary word in at least three of the questions.

3. Make an appointment to interview your chosen person. If possible, interview him or her in person while recording the discussion or taking careful notes. Alternatives include a phone interview and an e-mail interview.

4. Transcribe (write down) the interview. Write an introduction for the interview that tells why you wanted to ask this person questions and what you learned overall.

Master It: Use Words in Meaningful Ways

Your Choice

Directions: In this activity, you'll choose *one* of the following topics to write about. When you're finished, give a copy to your teacher. He or she will collect everyone's writing in a folder. When you have spare time in class, pull out someone's work, sit back, and enjoy a good read.

Writing Topics

> Write a biographical report on an individual and his or her *forte*.

> Write an article that introduces readers to various *genres* in literature or art.

> Write a skit in which a government soldier encounters a *guerrilla*—and not a shot is fired.

> Write a poem about a *nonchalant* person.

> Write an encyclopedia entry about the *orangutan*.

> Write a news report about a *regime*.

> Write a tourism brochure for a state or region, and mention *silos*.

> Write an informative article on *sloops*.

> Write a short story set on a *veranda*.

> Write a letter to the editor about a controversy, and use the term *vice versa*.

> Get approval for a topic that you create based upon a vocabulary word.

Vocabulary Mini-Lesson: Words Come from Mythology

Besides foreign languages, an interesting source of English words is Greek and Roman mythology. Mythology is the collection of myths, or stories that were told and written long ago to explain how or why things were created. These stories usually involve gods and heroes. For example, in mythology there is a goddess of rainbows, Iris, and a god Apollo who drives the sun across the sky every day.

Many familiar words have their origin in people or creatures described in ancient myths. Consider, for example, the word *atlas*, meaning "a book of maps." In Greek mythology, the giant Atlas was forced by Zeus to hold the heavens on his shoulders. The memorable image of Atlas supporting Earth was often displayed on the front page of early geography books.

Words to Know: Vocabulary Lists and Activities

In this section, you'll study ten words that come from Greek and Roman myths. You'll learn the myths from which these words have arisen as well as the more modern uses of the words.

List 15   Words from Mythology

Read each word, its origin, what it means, and how it's used.

Word	Its Origin	What It Means	How It's Used
chimera *(n)* ki-MEER-uh	in Greek mythology, a monster with a lion's head, a goat's body, and a serpent's tail	a made-up dream or illusion in the mind	My mom reassured my little sister that there was no monster under her bed; it was just a *chimera* of her vivid imagination.
iridescent *(adj)* ir-i-DEH-suhnt	In Greek mythology, *Iris* was the goddess of the rainbow.	having a rainbowlike display of colors	The glass ornament had an *iridescent* glow under the Christmas tree lights.
jovial *(adj)* JOH-vee-uhl	*Jove*, or Jupiter, was the chief Roman god.	filled with good humor; cheerful	Having received good news, Shira was in a *jovial* mood.
lethargy *(n)* LEH-ther-jee	from *Lethe*, a river in Greek mythology whose water was said to cause forgetfulness	the quality of being lazy, sluggish, and indifferent	Jordan was overcome with *lethargy*; he couldn't motivate himself to get off the couch and go for a run.
narcissistic *(adj)* nahr-suh-SIS-tik	In Greek mythology, *Narcissus* was a beautiful young man who fell in love with his own reflection.	overly concerned with oneself; self-centered; vain	Cal spent so much time looking at himself in the mirror, people said he was *narcissistic*.
nemesis *(n)* NEH-muh-sis	*Nemesis* was the Greek goddess of vengeance.	one who inflicts revenge; also, a formidable opponent	Superman's *nemesis* is the evil Lex Luthor.
pander *(v)* PAN-der	from *Pandarus*, an archer in the Trojan War who set up and encouraged a relationship between Cressida and Troilus	to accommodate or satisfy the desires or weaknesses of others	The car advertisement *panders* to the desires of men who want to look tough.
salutary *(adj)* SAL-yuh-ter-ee	from *Salus*, the Roman goddess of health	having a healthy or beneficial effect	If you're feeling sick, drinking plenty of liquids and getting a good night's sleep will have *salutary* effects.

continued

tantalize *(v)* TAN-teh-lize	In Greek mythology, *Tantalus* was a king condemned to stand in water that recedes when he tries to drink and beneath branches of fruit that stay out of his reach.	to tempt or torment, as by offering something desirable but withholding it	Luis was *tantalized* by the idea of going to the movies, but he knew he had to finish his report first.
titanic *(adj)* tie-TA-nik	In Greek mythology, the *Titans* were a race of giants.	having great size or power; colossal; immense	The *titanic* metal sculpture filled the museum's courtyard.

Own It: Develop Your Word Understanding

Yes, It Is—No, It's Not

Directions: Work with a partner to complete the activity. For each organizer, complete these steps:

1. *What It Is:* In this box, state what the key word means in your own words.
2. *What It's Not:* List antonyms, expressions with an opposite meaning to the key word, or things/ideas that someone may confuse with the key word. For example, *jovial* is not sad; a *nemesis* is not an ally.
3. *Examples:* List examples of the key word. For instance, what expensive product *tantalizes* you? What is something in your home that is *iridescent*?
4. *Memory Cue:* Sketch a simple illustration to help you remember the word's meaning.

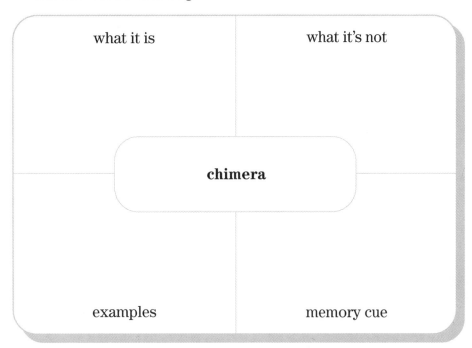

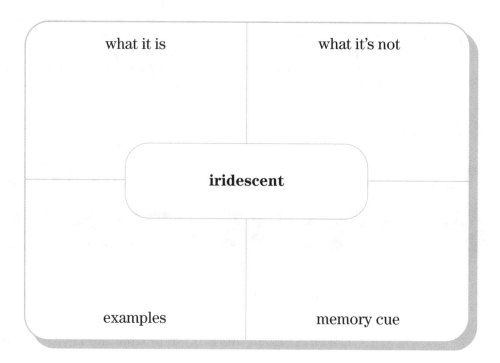

what it is

what it's not

iridescent

examples

memory cue

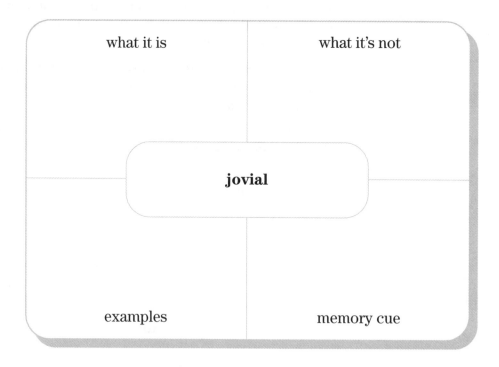

what it is

what it's not

jovial

examples

memory cue

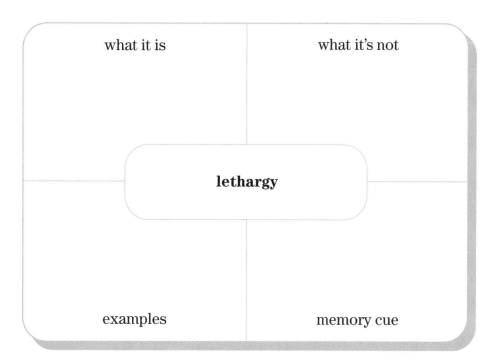

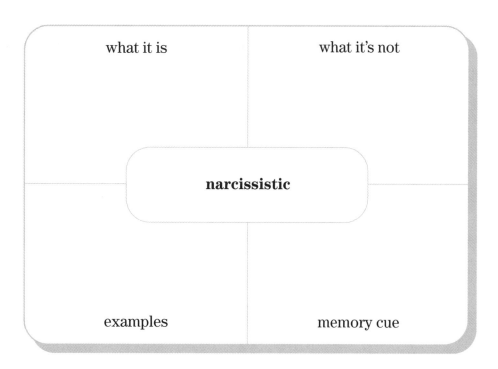

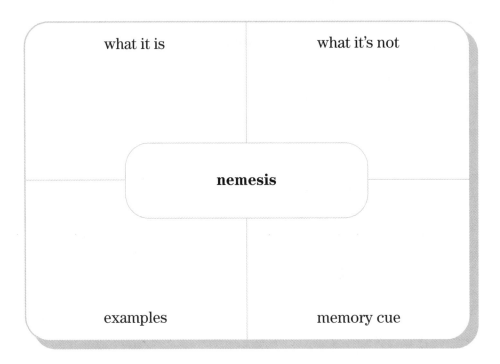

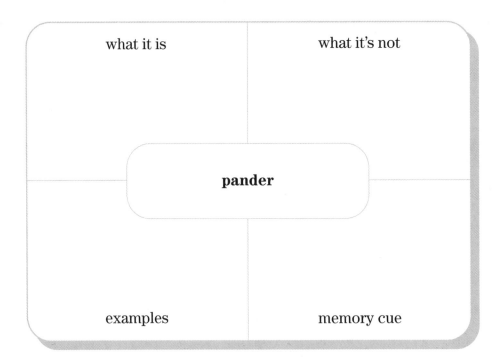

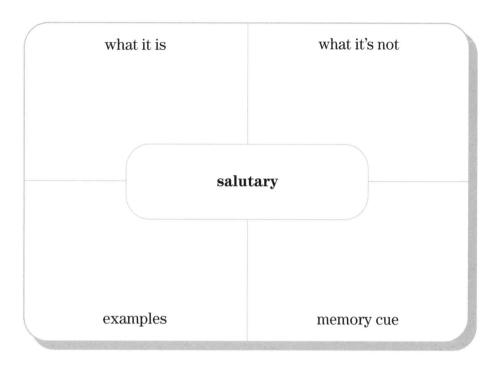

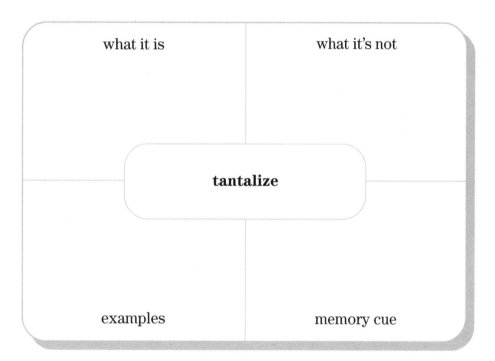

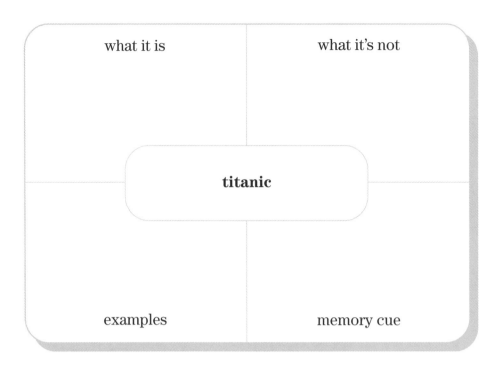

what it is	what it's not
titanic	
examples	memory cue

Sometimes I am overcome with <u>lethargy</u> by the end of a long school day, and I have no energy to do anything. I know that getting more sleep would have a <u>salutary</u> effect on my health, but it's hard to go to bed early when I have such a <u>titanic</u> amount of work to do! Yawn!

Link It: Make Word-to-World Connections

Visiting Celebrity

Directions: Imagine that Jove, Iris, Narcissus, Nemesis, Pandarus, Salus, Tantalus, or a Titan is coming to visit your school. What do you think this "celebrity" would say to students? What might be the reason for the visit?

Create a poster announcing the upcoming visit of one of these characters. Your poster should inform students of the character's visit, the purpose of the event, and why students will want to attend. As an added challenge, on your poster use the vocabulary word that is derived from the character's name.

When your poster is finished, display it in a classroom exhibit.

Master It: Use Words in Meaningful Ways

That Was Then. This Is Now

Directions: If myths were written about modern-day people, who would be the good-natured ruler? Who would be infamous for his or her vanity, and who would gain fame as a nemesis? Who would be lazy, who would tantalize, and who would be a titan in sports or entertainment?

Choose one of the eight mythological characters (Jove, Iris, Narcissus, Nemesis, Pandarus, Salus, Tantalus, or a Titan) and identify a modern-day person who is similar. Write a three-paragraph essay in which you

> ❯ introduce the Greek character and the modern-day person and tell how they are similar

> ❯ tell how the Greek character inspired the modern-day vocabulary word

Vocabulary Mini-Lesson: Words Come from the Names of People and Places

Did you know that the word *braille* comes from Louis *Braille*, the blind French teacher who created it? Such a word that comes from, or is based on, the name of a real or imaginary person is called an *eponym*. *Volt*, named for Italian physicist Alessandro Volta, is another example, as is *guillotine*, named for Joseph Guillotin, a French doctor who proposed its use for executions.

Many other common words get their names from people and places. Some are obvious—like *pasteurize*, named after Louis Pasteur, the French chemist who devised the process. Others may surprise you.

ords to Know: Vocabulary Lists and Activities

The words on the following list are named after famous people from different time periods or specific locations.

List 16 Words from the Names of People and Places

Read each word, what it means, its origin, and how it's used. Are you familiar with any of the people or places explained in the Origin column?

Word	What It Means	Its Origin	How It's Used
boycott *(v)* BOY-kot	to join with others to refuse to deal with, purchase, or use	named for Charles Boycott, a 19th-century land agent in Ireland whose tenants refused to deal with him	Commuters threatened to *boycott* the railroad if fares increased.
cashmere *(n)* KAZH-meer	fine wool obtained from goats of the Kashmir region of southern Asia	named after Cashmere, or Kashmir, the region in Asia	Wayne is wearing a *cashmere* sweater.
cologne *(n)* kuh-LONE	a perfumed liquid	named after Cologne, Germany, where it was manufactured	Mom loves the scent of the *cologne* we bought her for Mother's Day.
denim *(n)* DEH-nuhm	a sturdy, durable fabric, used to make jeans and other clothing	from *de Nîmes*, meaning "of Nîmes"; Nîmes is the French city where the fabric was first made	Hannah is wearing a jacket of blue *denim*.
epicure *(n)* EH-pi-kyoor	someone who is devoted to good food and drink	from Epicurus, a Greek philosopher who thought pleasure was the highest good	Melinda is an *epicure*; she always serves her guests the best food and drink.
galvanize *(v)* GAL-vuh-nize	to stimulate, as if by electric shock; excite; rouse	named for Luigi Galvani, an 18th-century Italian scientist	The mayor's proposal to raise taxes *galvanized* citizens to action.
mesmerize *(v)* MEZ-muh-rize	to hypnotize; captivate; fascinate	named for Franz Anton Mesmer, early 19th-century German physician who practiced hypnotism	We were *mesmerized* by the city lights twinkling in the distance.

continued

paparazzi *(n, plural)* pah-puh-RAHT-see	photographers who aggressively follow celebrities in order to take candid pictures	The singular form is *paparazzo*, which was the name of the photographer in *La Dolce Vita*, a 1960 movie by Italian film director Federico Fellini.	Witnesses said that *paparazzi* on motorcycles nearly forced the actor's car off the road.
rhinestone *(n)* RINE-stone	a bright, colorless artificial gem often made of glass	from French *caillou du Rhin*, meaning "pebble of the Rhine." These stones were originally made near Strasburg, Germany, located on the Rhine River.	Lydia wore a princess costume for the school play, with glittering *rhinestones* in the crown.
silhouette *(n)* sih-lih-WET	an outline of a figure; also, a profile portrait	named after Étienne de Silhouette, an 18th-century French finance minister, perhaps because silhouettes were less costly to make than painted portraits, a mocking reference to Silhouette's unpopular financial policies	The lamp cast a *silhouette* of the cat on the window shade.

Own It: Develop Your Word Understanding

Exploring Key Words

Directions: Use the following organizer to explore each vocabulary word. In the middle column, write your own explanation of the word's meaning. In the right-hand column, draw or write a cue to help you remember the word's meaning. If your teacher approves, work with a partner.

Key Word	My Personal Explanation of This Word's Meaning	Memory Cue
boycott		
cashmere		

continued

cologne		
denim		
epicure		
galvanize		
mesmerize		
paparazzi		
rhinestone		
silhouette		

Link It: Make Word-to-World Connections

In My Opinion

Directions: Chances are, you have an opinion related to one ore more of the vocabulary words. For instance, in your opinion, should people boycott stores that sell fur? Is cashmere overpriced or overrated? Do some people at school wear too much cologne?

First, as a class, brainstorm opinionated topics using the vocabulary words. Then, on a slip of paper, write one opinion you have, using a vocabulary word in the sentence. Your teacher will collect everyone's opinions and read them aloud one by one. Your teacher will pause so that students can agree or disagree with the opinion.

Master It: Use Words in Meaningful Ways

Class Mag

Directions: In this activity, you'll help create a magazine that showcases vocabulary words derived from proper nouns. Working with a partner, follow these steps:

1. Your teacher will assign a vocabulary word to you (or let you choose one). Your job is to create one magazine page that showcases this word. Here are some ideas:

   > create an advertisement

   > present a slogan (for example, "Boycott fur retailers")

   > write and illustrate an article (how-to, informative, etc.)

   > write and illustrate a short story, poem, or skit

   > use examples of a vocabulary word (for instance, denim, rhinestones, or silhouettes) to create artwork on a page, perhaps to showcase an inspiring quote, a slogan, a short how-to project, or the like

2. To create your magazine page, use neatly written or printed text, your own artwork, magazine cutouts, or other materials.

3. Your teacher will assemble everyone's page into a finished magazine by using a folder with brads, staples, or another method. The magazine will be available for you to read when you have spare time during class.

Wrapping Up: Review What You've Learned

Here's a brief summary of what you've studied in this chapter.

> Many familiar words come from foreign languages. They have been added to English over the centuries and are still being added today. These words may not seem foreign, either because their form has changed or because we are so used to hearing them.

> Just as English borrows from other languages, so do other languages borrow from English.

> Words often trace their origin back through two or more languages.

> Many words have their origin in people or creatures described in Greek and Roman mythology.

> Some common words are based on the names of famous people and places.

> A word that comes from, or is based on, the name of a real or imaginary person is called an *eponym*.

Chapter Review Exercises

 Flaunt It: Show Your Word Understanding

In the following exercises, you'll demonstrate your understanding of each vocabulary word. You will use vocabulary words, or forms of the words, to complete sentences and to write sentences of your own.

A   Word Bank

Directions: Choose a word from the box to complete each sentence. Write the word on the line provided. Each word may be used only once.

> connoisseur   encore   regime   titanic   silhouette
>   coup d'état   fiasco   vice versa   paparazzi   jovial

1. My sister's first effort to prepare dinner alone was a/an _____ but she is determined to become a chef.

2. In the dim room, a lamp cast Grandma's _____ against the wall.

3. In a/an _____, William of Orange overthrew James II in England in 1688.

4. Next to the five-pound toy poodle, the Great Dane looked _____.

5. The singer happily performed a/an _____, even though her voice was becoming hoarse.

6. As a/an _____ of seafood, I can recommend Deep Blue Seafood House for your special birthday dinner.

7. Because Danny is always so _____, I wonder if he sometimes hides feelings of sadness or anger.

8. The new _____ in the tiny nation is attracting worldwide press coverage.

9. Should we go to the beach first and then visit Aunt Tilly, or _____?

10. Some _____ have sold photographs of celebrities for more than a hundred thousand dollars.

B **Sentence Completion**

Directions: Circle the letter of the word that best completes each sentence.

11. The events of the previous week were _____, beginning with the elephant's wandering into my front yard.
    a. narcissistic   **b.** cliché
    c. iridescent   **d.** bizarre

12. At the _____, we bought jalapeños, tortillas, and *queso fresco*, which is a soft Mexican cheese.
    a. bodega   **b.** boutique
    c. veranda   **d.** dinghy

13. Many people in the neighborhood _____ Magic Cinema after it began showing X-rated movies.
    a. galvanized   **b.** boycotted
    c. tantalized   **d.** mesmerized

14. I left my new _____ sweater on my bed, and later I found my kitten snuggled in the folds of its softness.
    a. cashmere   **b.** denim
    c. nonchalant   **d.** rhinestone

15. As a nature photographer, Seth excels in taking photos such as this one of the _____ in its natural habitat.
    a. envoy   **b.** guerrilla
    c. sloop   **d.** orangutan

C **Writing**

Directions: Follow the directions to write sentences using vocabulary words. Write your sentences on a separate sheet of paper.

16. Use *silo* in a description of a farm.

17. Use *genre* in a statement about literature.

18. Use *forte* to tell something about yourself.

19. Use *nemesis* to tell something about sports.

20. Use *epicure* in a description of someone you know.

Activities à la Carte: Extend Your Word Knowledge

The activities on this page are presented à la carte, like items on a restaurant menu, meaning that you can choose from a variety of options. Your teacher may assign an activity or let you pick the one that tempts your appetite. If time allows, you might do more than one activity. All of the activities feature the same ingredient: **words derived from many sources**. Dig in!

My Eponym

If you could coin a new word based on your name, what would it be? What would this new word mean, and why would it derive from your name? Play around with your own name and create an eponym with a definition.

In My Dreams

Use vocabulary words to inspire dreams of yourself after high school or college. Do you want to become a *boutique* owner? A political *envoy*? An art *connoisseur*? A *sloop* builder? A *paparazzo*? Use your imagination and your dreams to create a future for yourself. Describe what you see in detail, either on paper or using a recording device. Then keep this "key" to your future with your personal belongings, to use as inspiration in setting and reaching goals.

Word Associations

Choose a vocabulary word (or words) and make a poster of words associated with the key word. For instance, use *dinghy* and *sloop* to inspire a poster explaining types of small sailing vessels. Use *encore* to inspire a poster introducing theater terms. Useful information to include for each word is a pronunciation guide, a definition, and an example of usage. You may also want to include pictures or other extras to entice readers.

 ## English Without Borders

In this chapter, you learned some "English" words borrowed directly from other languages, such as *bodega* and *cliché*. Now, turn the tables. Look for English words that are used in other languages.

A librarian can help you start your search. Based on your research, make a list of ten key English words that are useful for foreigners to know.

Telling Stories

Choose a Greek or Roman myth that younger kids would enjoy. Arrange with a teacher or librarian to present this myth to an elementary school class. Practice telling or reading the myth aloud (you could research tips for reading aloud). If possible, prepare at least one visual such as a poster or illustrations to grab your listeners' interest. If you enjoy the spotlight, perhaps you are destined for a career as an entertainer, teacher, or public speaker.

A Bizarre Bazaar?

Four of the words in this chapter have homophones: words that are pronounced the same but have different spellings and meanings.

> Write a sentence that uses the words *gorilla* and *guerrilla*.

> Write a sentence that explains how a *bazaar* can be *bizarre*.

> Write a sentence that uses the words *forte* and *fort*.

> Write a sentence that tells how a *chimaera* could be a *chimera*. (You will need a dictionary for this.)

One of a Kind—or One of Many?

Just how special are the words listed in this chapter? When people need to use the exact right word, do these words stand out as one of a kind? Or are they one of many equally useful choices? Develop your opinion on this issue by looking up vocabulary words in a thesaurus. Does each vocabulary word have synonyms? Are the synonyms equally precise, expressive, or unique? Overall, do you think English is richer because of words derived from other languages and proper nouns, or simply more cluttered?

Learning New and Special Words

6

W e all live in the same world: planet Earth. However, we also occupy our own unique worlds, made up of personal experiences and knowledge. When we study specific subjects or pursue careers, we enter other worlds— the world of science or technology, for instance, or the medical or legal world. All of these worlds have specialized words associated with them. In this chapter, you'll learn words from some of these worlds, and you'll add words to the vocabulary of *your* world.

Objectives

In this chapter, you will learn

> How and why our language expands

> New words from technology, science, medicine, and law

Sneak Peek: Preview the Lesson

The Best of All Worlds

Think about your world and your language. When you're with friends and family, what words and expressions do you use that "the outside world" may not use? Write some of these words in the circle on the next page labeled "my world."

Next, read the words in the outer circles. These are some of the words that you'll study in this chapter. Do you already know any of these words? If any words fit into your world, write them in the center circle. Chances are, your personal world already shares elements with at least one other world!

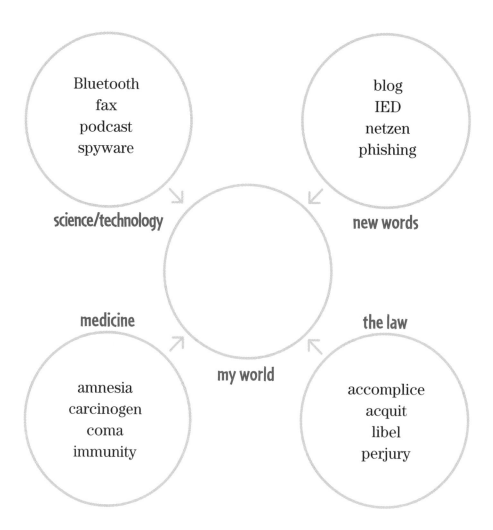

Vocabulary Mini-Lesson: How Our Language Expands

Our language is constantly growing and changing. New words are added, and old words take on new or changed meanings. Consider how computer technology has expanded the meaning of familiar words. Not too long ago, someone looking through books or magazines would be called a *browser*. Now when you hear that word you probably think of the computer software that's used to access the Internet. And how about *cookies*? No, not the kind you eat. Present-day *cookies* are small files stored on a computer that contain information about the user. And, of course, a *virus* is no longer just a cause of disease. It refers to a destructive computer program.

Sometimes new words are formed by blending other words or word parts. For example, *ginormous* combines letters from *gigantic* and *enormous*. *Cybercafe*, *cyberspace*, and *cybercrime* combine familiar words with the prefix *cyber-*, which means "relating to computers." Other words and phrases enter our language through technology and science, such as *text messaging, wireless, GPS* (short for *global positioning system*), *space shuttle,* and *global warming.*

Words to Know: Vocabulary Lists and Activities

This section contains technology and science words and new words from culture and society.

 Technology and Science Words

Read each word, what it means, and how it's used.

Word	What It Means	How It's Used
bioweapon *(n)* BIE-oh-WEH-puhn	(short for *biological weapon*) a harmful biological agent, such as a disease-spreading microorganism, used as a weapon	Soldiers may wear protective gear to protect themselves against *bioweapons* on the battlefield.
Bluetooth *(n)* BLEW-tooth	wireless technology for interconnecting electronic devices	*Bluetooth*-enabled products make communication easier at home and at work.
fax *(v, n)* faks	(short for *facsimile*) to transmit (a copy of a document) electronically over a telephone line	Courtney *faxed* the science notes she had taken in class to her study partner.
hologram *(n)* HAH-luh-gram	a three-dimensional photographic image produced by means of a laser	Because it is so difficult to copy *holograms*, these images are often used for security purposes on credit cards.
malware *(n)* MAL-ware	software designed to damage or disturb a computer's normal functioning (*mal-* is a Latin prefix meaning "bad")	The *malware* destroyed everything on Tyrone's hard drive, and he had to reinstall all his programs.
nanotechnology *(n)* nah-no-tek-NAH-luh-jee	the design and production of microscopic electronic devices built from atoms and molecules	Using *nanotechnology*, scientists hope to create a camera tiny enough to be injected into a blood vessel.
netroots *(n)* NET-roots	political activism conducted over the Internet, especially via blogs	The senator began a *netroots* campaign to get the attention of young people across America.

continued

podcast *(n)* pod-kast	(blend of *iPod* and *broadcast*) a digital file distributed over the Internet to be downloaded onto computers and media players	Andrew listens to *podcasts* of his favorite radio show.
spyware *(n)* SPAHY-wair	software that enables someone to obtain information about a person's computer activities without that person's knowledge	Some software companies have used *spyware* to collect personal information about customers.
webinar *(n)* WEB-ih-nahr	a live educational seminar or presentation on the Internet, during which participants can usually ask questions	I attended a *webinar* on how to get into the acting business after college.

Own It: Develop Your Word Understanding

Accept or Reject?

Directions: In this activity, you'll try to spot fake definitions of the vocabulary words. Here's how the activity works:

1. Your teacher will assign you and a partner one of the vocabulary words. On an index card, write your names and the word you received. On the back of the card, write a *correct* definition of the word and an *incorrect* definition that you make up. (Label each definition.) Make sure that your incorrect definition is still related to the correct one, so that the wrong answer is not too obvious.

2. Your teacher will mix everyone's cards together in a box.

3. Your teacher will pull out a card and read the vocabulary word aloud. Then he or she will read *one* of the definitions on the card.

4. Your teacher will ask for a show of hands to indicate whether you *accept* or *reject* the definition. Be prepared to defend your vote!

Link It: Make Word-to-World Connections

Thinking of You

Directions: Technology and science words can seem intimidating to people. Their fear can stand in the way of learning the new words. Do you know someone like this? Help this person by personally explaining a few technology and science words. Here's what to do.

1. Review the list of vocabulary words. As you do so, think about someone you know who may be unfamiliar with some of these words. Choose *three* words to work with.

2. Write a letter to the person you chose. In the letter, mention that you are studying technology and science words. Suggest that this person may like to know about a few of these words. Then explain the meaning of each word and give an example of how the person might use it in his or her own life.

3. Share a copy of the letter with your teacher. Whether or not you send the letter to its addressee is up to you!

Master It: Use Words in Meaningful Ways

Have a Conversation

Directions: In this activity, you and your classmates will have a conversation with your teacher. The goal is to use as many vocabulary words as possible during the conversation. Here's how it works:

1. Your teacher will divide the class into teams.

2. Your teacher will get a conversation started by reading one of these prompts:

   > I wonder if the world is better off with, or without, technology.

   > I wonder if any of these terms will become outdated in the next 20 years.

   > I wonder which of these things will have the biggest impact on the lives of people in this room.

   > How do you think science will impact technology in the next 20 years?

   > What country do you think will take over being the main technological developer in the future and why?

3. Raise your hand to signal that you want to share in the conversation. Then state a sentence that uses a vocabulary word *and* that makes sense in the conversation.

4. When one or more conversations are finished, your teacher will add up each team's points and declare a winner.

List 18   New Words and Meanings

These words don't fall under one specific topic but have entered into our language due to new trends, issues, problems, or products in society. Read each word, what it means, and how it's used.

Word	What It Means	How It's Used
agritourism (n) ah-gri-TOOR-i-zuhm	the touring or visiting of farms or agricultural areas, usually with some participation in farm activities	At first I was bummed when my mom said we'd be going on an *agritourism* vacation in Vermont, but helping make maple syrup was actually really cool.
baby boomer (n) BAY-bee BOO-mer	someone born during a period of increased birth rates (a "baby boom"), especially a person born during the period after World War II, 1946–1964	The millions of *baby boomers* in the United States continue to have a dramatic effect on American culture.
biodiesel (n) BIE-oh-DEE-zuhl	fuel that is like diesel fuel but is made out of vegetable substances like soybean oil	Some new car models use *biodiesel* fuel.
blog (n) blahg	(short for *Weblog*) a journal or diary posted online by the writer	Benjamin updates his *blog* every day, adding his thoughts and comments about daily events.
dot-com (n) dot-KOM	(from the use of ".com" as part of a Web address) a company that markets its products or services mainly through the Internet	Many *dot-coms* begin with promising ideas but cannot attract enough customers to stay in business.
downsize (v) DOUN-sahyz	to reduce in size; usually means to reduce the number of employees in a business	Fifteen people lost their jobs when the advertising agency had to *downsize*.
identity theft (n) eye-DEN-ti-tee theft	the illegal use of another person's personal information for the purpose of financial gain	Police arrested the man for *identity theft* when they found stolen credit card numbers in his possession.
IED (n) I-E-D	(short for *improvised explosive device*) a crudely made bomb	When the roadside *IED* exploded, several soldiers were injured.
netizen (n) NET-uh-zuhn	(blend of *Internet* and *citizen*) a person who spends a substantial amount of time on the Internet	*Netizens* go online to share their ideas with others.
phishing (n) FISH-ing	an attempt to trick a computer user into revealing confidential personal information, which is then stolen and used illegally	The e-mail asked Amanda to enter her Social Security number, but she recognized the fake message as *phishing*.

Own It: Develop Your Word Understanding

Phishing for Details

Directions: Write your answer to each question on the lines provided. When you respond, use the vocabulary word in a complete sentence.

1. Who is a person you admire who is a *baby boomer*?

_____

2. Name a person whose *blog* you'd read if you knew he or she wrote one.

_____

3. What have you purchased (or wished you could purchase) from a *dot-com*?

_____

4. What is one thing you can do to prevent *identity theft*?

_____

5. What type of news story would most likely mention an *IED*?

_____

6. Do you know a *netizen*? Or have you read about one, or seen one in a movie? Explain.

_____

7. What is one type of information that a criminal may use *phishing* to find out?

_____

Link It: Make Word-to-World Connections

Career Paths

Directions: In a small group, discuss how each vocabulary word relates to one or more career paths. For instance, how might *phishing* relate to the career of a lawyer or a police officer? How might a science teacher be a *netizen*?

Use the organizer below to record links between vocabulary words and career paths. Then, in a class discussion, explain some links that your group discussed.

Links Between Vocabulary Words and Career Paths	
agritourism	baby boomer
biodiesel	blog
dot-com	downsize
identity theft	IED
netizen	phishing

Master It: Use Words in Meaningful Ways

Blog

Directions: Write a blog post inspired by one of the vocabulary words. The purpose of your post may be to entertain, to inform, to persuade, or to express—it's your choice. For instance, you might entertain readers with a story about a *netizen*. You might express your emotional reaction when a family member became a victim of *identity theft*. In selecting a topic, use your imagination, and consider sharing ideas with a friend.

Your teacher will collect copies of each person's blog posts in a folder. When you have a few spare minutes in class, pull out a post and read it.

Words to Know: Vocabulary Lists and Activities

Technology and science terms are not the only special words in our varied language. The fields of medicine and law are filled with words that people use in everyday conversation, hear on television and in the movies, and read in newspapers and magazines. The first list in this section contains ten medical words that are important not just for doctors but are useful for the average person to know. The second list contains legal words that are also used on a regular basis.

List 19   Medical Words

Read each word, what it means, and how it's used.

Word	What It Means	How It's Used
amnesia *(n)* am-NEE-zhuh	loss of memory, usually as a result of an accident or illness	After the car accident, Isaiah suffered from *amnesia* and had difficulty remembering basic details about his own life.
benign *(adj)* bi-NINE	not threatening to health (particularly: not becoming cancerous)	Luckily, the spot on her arm turned out to be *benign* and was not skin cancer.
carcinogen *(n)* kahr-SI-nuh-juhn	a substance that causes cancer	People should not smoke, because tobacco is a known *carcinogen*.

continued

chronic *(adj)* KRAH-nik	lasting a long time or recurring often (The root *chron* appears on List 9, page 59, and the suffix *-ic* appears on List 7, page 39.)	Although asthma is a *chronic* disease, medication can control it.
coma *(n)* KOH-muh	a state of prolonged unconsciousness caused by injury or disease	The athlete suffered a blow to the head, which left him in a *coma*.
immunity *(n)* i-MYOO-ni-tee	the body's ability to resist germs	Someone who eats a healthy diet and exercises regularly will generally have greater *immunity* to disease than someone who doesn't.
incision *(n)* in-SIH-zhuhn	a cut or gash; especially a cut made for surgical purposes	After the operation, the doctor stitched up the *incision*.
inconclusive *(adj)* in-kuhn-KLOO-siv	leading to no conclusion or definite result	The blood tests were *inconclusive*; doctors still weren't sure whether or not she had diabetes.
inflammation *(n)* in-fluh-MAY-shuhn	redness, swelling, or pain of body tissue, usually as a result of injury or irritation	I suffered from some painful *inflammation* around my right knee after I fell down at the skating rink.
transfusion *(n)* trans-FYOO-zhuhn	transferring blood from one person to another	Having lost a great deal of blood, the accident victim needed a *transfusion*.

Own It: Develop Your Word Understanding

Look It Up

Directions: Work with a partner to complete the activity. Here's what to do:

1. Look up each vocabulary word in an encyclopedia, dictionary, or other reference source. Your goal? To gain a broader understanding of the word. For instance, when you look up *carcinogen*, you may find examples of different carcinogens, or you may find out what cancer is. Both pieces of information will help you understand *carcinogen* better.

2. Fill in the table by writing and/or drawing a piece of new information about each word.

3. In a class discussion, share some of the facts you learned.

Key Word	Something New I Learned About This Word
amnesia	
benign	
carcinogen	
chronic	
coma	
immunity	
incision	
inconclusive	
inflammation	
transfusion	

Link It: Make Word-to-World Connections

Asked and Answered

Directions: In this activity, you will ask a question about a vocabulary word *and* answer classmates' questions. Here's how the activity works:

1. Skim the list of vocabulary words and their definitions. What questions come to mind about one or more of the words?

2. On a slip of paper, write a question using one of the vocabulary words. For instance, you might ask, "Is secondhand cigarette smoke a *carcinogen*?" or "How can I boost my *immunity* to colds?"

3. Give your question to your teacher, who will mix together all the slips of paper.

4. Your teacher will pull out a question and read it aloud. If you know an answer, raise your hand and give an answer. Others may agree with your or add to what you say.

5. If your teacher reads a question and no one knows an answer, write the question down to use in the following activity.

Master It: Use Words in Meaningful Ways

Ask Me Again

Directions: Choose one unanswered question from the activity above and find an answer to it. You might consult someone with medical knowledge, such as a school nurse, a pharmacist in a local drugstore, your family doctor, or a health teacher. Other sources of medical information include medical encyclopedias, health textbooks, hospital newsletters, and trustworthy Web sites such as that of the American Lung Association.

Based on information you find, write an answer to the question. Then read the question and your answer to the class.

List 20 Legal Words

Read each word, what it means, and how it's used.

Word	What It Means	How It's Used
accomplice (n) uh-KOM-plis	someone who knowingly participates in the commission of a crime	The bank robber's *accomplice* waited outside in a car.
acquit (v) uh-KWIT	to declare to be innocent of a crime	The accused man was *acquitted* because there was not enough evidence against him.
allege (v) uh-LEJ	to state or claim something before proving or without proving	The witness *alleged* that the man in the blue knit cap stole the young woman's wallet.

continued

defendant *(n)* di-FEN-duhnt	a person sued by another or accused of a crime	The *defendant* pleaded not guilty.
libel *(n)* LIE-buhl	a published or broadcast statement that is untrue and hurts a person's reputation	The actress sued the newspaper for *libel*, claiming their story was totally false.
perjury *(n)* PUR-juh-ree	making a false statement in a court of law while swearing it to be true	The witness who had told a lie was later charged with *perjury*.
plaintiff *(n)* PLAIN-tif	a person who brings a lawsuit against another person	The *plaintiff* claims that the defendant stole her computer.
prosecute *(v)* PRAH-si-kyoot	to bring legal action against for the committing of a crime or breaking of a law	The defendant will be *prosecuted* for his crime and could face five years in prison.
slander *(n)* SLAN-der	an oral statement that is untrue and hurts a person's reputation	The candidate accused her opponent of *slander*, saying that the charges made in a speech were all lies.
testimony *(n)* TES-tuh-moh-nee	oral statements sworn to be true in a court of law	*Testimony* by three witnesses helped to convict Mr. Adams of fraud.

Own It: Develop Your Word Understanding

Mix and Match

Directions: In this activity, you will mingle with classmates, trying to match vocabulary words with their definitions. Here's what to do.

1. Your teacher will write each vocabulary word on an index card. On separate cards, he or she will write the definitions. Then the cards will be jumbled together in a box.

2. You pull one card from the box. You'll have either a vocabulary word or a definition.

3. Move around the classroom to find the person who has the definition of your vocabulary word, or the word that goes with your definition.

4. In a class discussion, explain how easy or difficult it was to make the match. Which words or definitions made you think hard about whether they were a correct match? Which were easier to eliminate?

Link It: Make Word-to-World Connections

Need an Alibi?

Directions: We often use legal words in nonlegal settings. For instance, your mom may ask who your *accomplice* was in raiding the cookie jar. Or you may refer to a friend who is angry with you as "the *plaintiff.*"

In the first column of the table, give an example of how you could use each legal word in your everyday life. In a small group, share your examples. Then write other people's ideas in the third column.

Legal Word	Used in My Life	Ideas from Group
accomplice		
acquit		
allege		
defendant		
libel		
perjury		
plaintiff		

continued

prosecute		
slander		
testimony		

My buddy Dylan asked me to be his <u>accomplice</u> and help him play an April Fool's joke on his brother. They always play harmless jokes on each other that day. His brother started that precedent on April 1st years ago, when he swapped Dylan's lunch with fake plastic food. Dylan hadn't noticed and tried to take a bite! It was pretty funny.

Master It: Use Words in Meaningful Ways

Long Arm of the Law

Directions: If you formed a student court of law at your school, how would it work? Would *libel* or *slander* be cause for trial? Who could be called to give *testimony*? Who would be the judge? The jury? What would happen if a *defendant* were found guilty?

1. In a small group, brainstorm ideas based on these and other questions.

2. Together, prepare a description of the ideal student court of law. (To divide up the work, you can break the description into sections.) Be sure to use vocabulary words!

3. Present your recommendation to the class. You might choose to use one spokesperson from your group, or to take turns speaking.

4. Reflect on what you heard. How is your ideal court similar to those of other groups? How is it different? After hearing other ideas, would you change anything in your own court of law?

Wrapping Up: Review What You've Learned

Here's a brief summary of what you've studied in this chapter.

> The English language is constantly growing and changing. New words are added, while old words take on new or changed meanings.

> Some new words are formed by blending other words. Other words enter our language through technology and science.

> There are many medical and legal words that people use in everyday conversation, hear on television and in the movies, and read in newspapers and magazines.

Flaunt It: Show Your Word Understanding

In the following exercises, you'll demonstrate your understanding of each vocabulary word. You will use vocabulary words, or forms of the words, to complete sentences and to write sentences of your own.

A Word Bank

Directions: Choose a word from the box to complete each sentence. Write the word on the line provided. Each word may be used only once.

> immunity   carcinogens   plaintiff   coma   nanotechnology
> testimony   transfusions   chronic   acquit   netizens

1. One way to guard against cancer is to avoid exposure to _____.

2. After waking from a _____, the patient said that she did not remember how she had been injured.

3. According to his _____ in court, my client was out of town on the night that a fire destroyed the Taco Hut.

4. My dad's sister takes a new course at the local college very year; he calls her a _____ student.

5. Thanks to many generous blood donors, the hospital was able to make all needed _____ this week.

6. The young man cried with joy when the jury voted to _____ him of the charge of selling company secrets.

7. A specialist in _____ works with individual atoms to build microscopic devices such as electronic circuits.

8. Not getting enough sleep will lower your _____ to colds and flus.

9. As a courtesy to fellow _____, do not use all capitals when typing messages in chat rooms.

10. My cousin, a landscaper, is the _____ in a lawsuit filed against a woman who refused to pay him for his work.

B   Sentence Completion

Directions: Circle the letter of the word that best completes each sentence.

11. Students were angry when they learned that school officials had installed _____ on all school computers.

     a. holograms   **b.** podcasts

     c. spyware   **d.** nanotechnology

12. After researching the 1950s, thirteen-year-old Colin concluded that _____ grew up in a world quite different from his own world.

     a. dot-coms   **b.** baby boomers

     c. netizens   **d.** Bluetooth

13. Many companies accept orders sent by _____.

     a. fax   **b.** blog

     c. IED   **d.** phishing

14. After her wallet was stolen, Mom signed up for a class on the prevention of _____.

     a. defendants   **b.** bioweapons

     c. identity theft   **d.** accomplices

15. One of the candidates for mayor told interviewers lies about his opponents; as a result, he was charged with _____.

     a. perjury   **b.** immunity

     c. libel   **d.** slander

C   Writing

Directions: Follow the directions to write sentences using vocabulary words. Write your sentences on a separate sheet of paper.

16. Describe a product that might appeal to *baby boomers*.

17. Use *blog* as the subject of a sentence.

18. Use *accomplice* to tell about a crime.

19. Use *podcast* in a friendly command.

20. Use *phishing* to express a warning to a friend.

Activities à la Carte: Extend Your Word Knowledge

The activities on this page are presented à la carte, like items on a restaurant menu, meaning that you can choose from a variety of options. Your teacher may assign an activity or let you pick the one that tempts your appetite. If time allows, you might do more than one activity. All of the activities feature the same ingredient: **new and special words**. Dig in!

Do the Math

Math can help information come alive. If you enjoy charting statistics, drawing pie charts, or finding percentages, then grab a pencil! Choose a research topic inspired by a vocabulary word. Do the research, do the math, and create a visual showing the results. Then share it with your class.

Rock My World

If you are musically inclined, set some words from this chapter to music. You can rock them, rap them, croon them, chant them, or give them the blues. It's up to you!

Tell Me a Tale

Write a short story about a student brought to trial in a teen court. You can use the story to explore an issue that intrigues you, such as how exactly would a teen court work? What happens if someone is falsely accused? What happens if someone is guilty but is acquitted due to lack of evidence? Can a teen court make a difference in teens' lives?

Show-and-Tell

Do you miss the good old days of show and tell, back when you were little? Well, it's time to revive that practice. Your assignment? Bring in a *person* to show and tell about. This person must be connected in some way to one or more vocabulary words in this chapter.

 ## Word Patrol

If you know a second language, search that language for new words and meanings. Can you identify new words in that language that don't have English translations? Or old words that have taken on new meanings? What about the new words and meanings in this chapter—do any of them translate into the other language and keep the same meaning? Use your findings to draw conclusions or make predictions about the two languages.

Mock Trial

Did you enjoy the Long Arm of the Law activity in this chapter (page 129)? Get some friends together and stage a mock trial. Use ideas from the activity to give structure to your trial. You can use the trial to draw attention to a rule at school that you think is necessary—or ridiculous.

Brave New World

Did your study of new and specialized words spark an interest in a world outside your own? Find a way to explore this world. You could interview a professional, research articles and books, watch a video, or read news coverage. Based on your findings, prepare an oral report for your class. Your purpose is to persuade class-mates that this world has a place for them in it. (As an alternative, if you already know a field you'd like to enter in the future, you can research the kinds of specialized vocabulary you'll need to learn for this world. Share your findings with the class.)

Learning Words from Context

7

Objectives

In this chapter, you will learn

> How context clues can help you determine the meanings of unknown words

> Six ways to use context clues

> Words from literature, history, science, and history passages that you'll figure out yourself using context clues

Has someone ever caused trouble for you by taking your words out of context—by using them in a different scenario than you intended? Maybe you were describing your best friend, and you said she was crazy. In the context of the conversation, *crazy* meant "thrilling and entertaining." However, suppose someone overheard you and told your best friend, "Guess who thinks you're crazy?" Taking this one word out of context can completely change its meaning.

Just like spoken words, written words depend on context for full and accurate meaning. In this chapter, you'll study the most common types of context clues. You'll learn to use these clues to determine word meanings. You may want to add some of the fascinating words you study to your permanent vocabulary.

Sneak Peek: Preview the Lesson

Student Teacher

What do you know already about context clues? Can you explain what a context clue is? Can you give an example of a type of context clue? In a class discussion, teach classmates what you know about context clues. If you have used context clues before, describe what you did. In addition, listen to what other people say about context clues. Finally, complete the sentence at the top of the next page.

After I complete this lesson, I hope to be able to

Vocabulary Mini-Lesson: How to Use Context Clues

As you're reading, you may encounter a word whose meaning you're not sure of. An author may use descriptive words that are new to you or whose meanings you've forgotten. Or an article on the Internet or in a magazine may contain unfamiliar scientific terms. In situations like these, context clues can help you figure out the meaning of the unknown words.

Context means the words or sentences that precede and follow a particular word. The word *context* comes from the Latin word *contexere*, meaning "to weave together."

Sometimes you need very little context to figure out a word, while other times you may have to consider a whole paragraph to find the clues needed to understand a word's meaning. Let's look at an example of how context clues work. Imagine that you see this news story on the Web.

> The young actor's arrival at The Paradise Hotel caused quite a scene at lunchtime today. Hundreds of screaming fans eager to catch a glimpse of the movie star besieged his limousine, blocking traffic in both directions and making it impossible for him to exit the vehicle. Police had to be called in to clear the crowds.

The word *besiege* may be unfamiliar to you. However, the detailed description helps you picture the scene: "hundreds of screaming fans . . . blocking traffic . . . impossible for him to exit the vehicle . . . clear the crowds." From these context clues, you can figure out that *besiege* means "surround or crowd around."

Context clues take various forms. For example, a writer may make a word's meaning clear by giving examples. Or a writer may provide a definition or an explanation of a term, as in a science textbook. Sometimes a writer suggests the meaning of a word by making a comparison. You'll see examples of all of these kinds of context clues and others in the following sections.

Six Ways to Use Context Clues

1. Examine the Descriptive Details

The details that a writer includes when describing something offer important clues to word meaning. Notice the descriptive details in the following passage. Can you figure out the meaning of the underlined word from these details?

The climb to the top of Eagle Mountain was the most <u>strenuous</u> hike I've ever taken. For three solid hours, we ascended the steep mountain. Often we had to cling to rocks and trees just to keep from tumbling backward. At the halfway point, the temperature reached 85 degrees under the fiery sun, and we had to stop every few minutes to drink water and catch our breath. Every muscle in my body was aching when we finally pulled our way up to the peak, but the view from the mountaintop was unforgettable.

Descriptive details suggest the meaning of *strenuous*. The mountain is very steep and takes three hours to climb. The hot sun is beating down. Every muscle is aching by the time the narrator reaches the top. Based on these context clues, you can conclude that *strenuous* means "requiring great effort or energy."

Here's another example. What descriptive details help you figure out the meaning of the underlined word in this passage?

On our way to Greenville, we must have taken a wrong turn because we ended up in the middle of nowhere. Hoping to get directions, we knocked on the door of the first cabin we came to. Even though we were strangers, the middle-aged couple who lived there were as <u>hospitable</u> as they could possibly be. They invited us inside, offered us a cold drink, and even packed up some freshly baked cookies for us to take along. Then they drew us a little map to help us find our way.

List three descriptive details that provide clues to the meaning of *hospitable*.

a. _____

b. _____

c. _____

Based on the context clues you listed, what do you think hospitable means? Write an explanation or definition.

_____

2. Look for an Explanation or Definition

Writers often explain or define a word when they use it. Look at these examples. What does the underlined word mean? How do you know?

Families that hope to send their children to college must plan ahead so that they can afford the <u>tuition</u>, the cost of instruction at the school of choice.

Based on the definition in the sentence, you can tell that *tuition* is

_____

Mrs. Jacobs told Dr. Welliver that her joints and muscles ached. In addition, the doctor noted that some of her joints and muscles were inflamed. He concluded that she was suffering from <u>rheumatism</u>.

Based on the description in the paragraph, what do you think *rheumatism* is?

_____

3. Search for Examples

Looking at the examples a writer gives can help you understand the meaning of an unfamiliar word. The examples may appear in the same sentence as the word or in a separate sentence.

Read the following sentence. It uses examples as clues to the meaning of *arachnids*.

> Unlike insects, <u>arachnids</u>, such as scorpions, spiders, and ticks, are wingless animals with four pairs of legs, only two main body parts, and no antennae.

What examples in the sentence help you figure out the meaning of *arachnids*?

a. _____

b. _____

c. _____

Based on the examples in the sentence, what do you think an *arachnid* is? Write an explanation or definition.

_____

_____

Now take a look at another passage that uses examples as context clues.

> My aunt Mary loves to quote <u>adages</u>. For example, when I was young, she always used to tell me, "Don't count your chickens before they're hatched." Another favorite of hers is, "When life gives you lemons, make lemonade."

What examples does the writer provide that help you figure out what an *adage* is?

a. _____

b. _____

Based on the examples, what do you think an *adage* is? Write an explanation or definition.

_____

_____

4. Look for a Synonym

A **synonym** is a word that means the same or almost the same as another word. For example, *frigid* and *icy* are synonyms for *cold*; *dull* and *tedious* are synonyms for *boring*. Synonyms can be helpful context clues.

Look at these examples. Can you find the synonyms of the underlined words?

Crossing the <u>torrid</u> desert, the travelers stopped often to rest. The burning sand stretched out endlessly before them, with no relief in sight.

What is a synonym of *torrid*? _____
Now that you know what *torrid* means, use it in a sentence of your own.

_____

_____

The rocket soared into the sky with such <u>velocity</u> that it was no more than a blur. The craft's amazing speed left spectators gasping.

What is a synonym of *velocity*? _____
Now that you know what *velocity* means, use it in a sentence of your own.

_____

_____

5. Look for a Comparison

Writers may suggest a word's meaning by comparing one thing to another. Often, the comparison uses the word *like* or *as*.

In the following sentence, to what is Blake's behavior compared? How does this comparison help you understand the underlined word?

> "Blake, your behavior is as <u>infantile</u> as a two-year-old's," Mom said. "It's time you grew up!"

In the sentence, Blake's behavior is compared to the behavior of

_____

How does the comparison help you understand the meaning of *infantile*?

_____

_____

What do you think *infantile* means?

_____

To what is the volcano's lava compared in the next sentence? (Hint: Look for the word *like*.) How does the comparison help you understand the underlined word?

> The <u>molten</u> lava poured down the side of the volcano like a river of fire.

In the sentence, the *molten* lava is compared to what?

_____

How does the comparison help you understand the meaning of *molten*?

_____

_____

What do you think *molten* means?

_____

6. Look for a Contrast

While a comparison shows how two things are similar, a contrast points out how they are different. Writers making a contrast often use one of these words: *but, however, although, while,* or *unlike.* Look at this example:

> Jasmine normally has an <u>amiable</u> disposition, but she may become grumpy when under stress.

The word *but* signals a contrast. Jasmine "normally has an *amiable* disposition." In contrast, "she may become grumpy when under stress." *Amiable,* in contrast with *grumpy,* means "agreeable, friendly."

Here's another example:

> Unlike his older brother, who is an <u>arrogant</u> young man, Jake is always humble.

Which word signals that the sentence will express a contrast?

_____

Which word expresses a contrast to *arrogant*? _____

Based on the contrast expressed in the sentence, what do you think *arrogant* means?

_____

Notice, too, that *amiable* and *grumpy* and *arrogant* and *humble* are antonym pairs. An **antonym** is a word that means the opposite of another word. Writers often use antonyms when they make a contrast.

> ### Tip
> When you encounter an unfamiliar word, combine your knowledge of word parts (Chapters 1–4) with your knowledge of context clues. The more hints to meaning you can find, the better able you will be to figure out the word.

Words to Know: Vocabulary Lists and Activities

Now you'll read nonfiction and literary passages and try using context clues to figure out word meanings. When you're done, you'll get a chance to check if your meanings are correct, and you'll study these new words.

Reading a Nonfiction Text

The following passage comes from a magazine article. As you read the passage, use context clues to try to figure out the meaning of the underlined words.

Why Do We Fight?

World War I was once thought to be "the war to end all wars." Yet, countless wars and military conflicts have occurred around the world since World War I ended nearly a century ago. Is war inevitable? Is armed conflict between people and nations truly un-avoidable? This question remains a persistent topic of debate, a subject that people have argued about for ages.

Most animals that hunt and kill have to do so in order to live. Their actions are a matter of survival. However, humans are among the few creatures on Earth who kill their own kind. While other animals kill for food, humans kill for different reasons.

Some scientists say that humans are naturally aggressive. These scientists maintain that aggression—hostile, threatening, or destructive behavior—is inborn. In other words, all people are born with a tendency to act aggressively. Other scientists dis-agree, declaring that humans do not have this propensity.

Dr. Louis Leakey, a British scientist who studied prehistoric peoples, argued that humans' aggressive behavior was not the result of human nature, but of civilization. Our primitive ances-tors killed animals for food, but Dr. Leakey found no evidence of warfare, or even murder, until about 40,000 years ago. That was about the time that people learned how to use fire.

Dr. Leakey believed that the use of fire made human life safer and more secure. Greater <u>security</u> enabled people to live longer, and the population increased. As more and more people began competing for the available <u>resources</u>, they started to fight one another for possessions and land. As humans became more civilized, they developed more and more destructive weapons. Today, these "civilized" people have weapons that are <u>devastating</u> enough to <u>eradicate</u> all life on Earth.

Write your definition of each word on the lines below. Then compare your definitions to those in List 21.

inevitable _____

_____

persistent _____

_____

survival _____

_____

aggression _____

_____

inborn _____

_____

propensity _____

_____

security _____

_____

resources _____

_____

devastating _____

_____

eradicate _____

_____

List 21 Words from a Nonfiction Text

Read each word, what it means, and how it's used. Were your definitions correct?

Word	What It Means	How It's Used
inevitable _(adj)_ i-NEV-i-tuh-buhl	not to be avoided; sure to happen; unavoidable	Alyssa knew that if she didn't study for the history test, it was _inevitable_ that she would fail.
persistent _(adj)_ per-SIS-tuhnt	continuing; ongoing	Dr. Burke gave Luis medicine for his _persistent_ cough.
survival _(n)_ ser-VIE-vuhl	staying alive; outlasting others	Our puppy's _survival_ depends on the care we give him.
aggression _(n)_ uh-GREH-shuhn	hostile, threatening, or destructive behavior	The president accused the neighboring nation of _aggression_ for sending troops across the border.
inborn _(adj)_ IN-BAWRN	in a person at birth; natural; instinctive	The child seemed to have _inborn_ musical talent.
propensity _(n)_ pruh-PEN-suh-tee	tendency; inclination	Sarah's _propensity_ for scientific analysis may lead her to a career in medical research.
security _(n)_ si-KYOOR-i-tee	freedom from danger; safety	The Secret Service works to ensure the president's _security_.
resources _(n)_ REE-sawr-sez	supplies that can meet a need; materials available for use	Despite the soldiers' limited _resources_, they managed to hold their position.
devastating _(adj)_ DE-vuh-stay-ting	destructive; damaging	The _devastating_ earthquake toppled numerous buildings.
eradicate _(v)_ i-RA-di-cate	to eliminate; wipe out	The pest control expert promised to _eradicate_ bugs from the house.

Own It: Develop Your Word Understanding

Share and Compare

Directions: Form a group of five people and assign each person two vocabulary words. For each of your two words, follow these steps:

1. **Compare definitions.** Compare the definition you wrote on page 144 or 145 with the definition given in List 21. If necessary, make corrections to your definition. To become familiar with this new word, read the passage again with the revised definition in mind.

2. **Identify context clues.** Look again at the context clues that helped you determine the word's meaning. Referring to the list below, identify the type(s) of context clues that helped you understand the word.

Types of Context Clues

> descriptive details
> explanation or definition
> examples
> synonym

> comparison
> contrast
> antonym

3. **Share and compare.** Practice saying your two vocabulary words aloud. Then share these words, along with your definitions, with your group. Tell what context clues helped you understand the words. Listen as others share their results and make revisions to your definitions if necessary.

Link It: Make Word-to-World Connections

A Mile in Your Shoes

Directions: In the table on the next page, you "visit" different places in your home and think about how vocabulary words relate to your life there. Answer the questions to express what it's like to "walk a mile in your shoes." Share your answers in a group or class discussion.

dining room: At the dining table, what topics of conversation are *inevitable*?	**family room:** What *persistent* behavior of a family member would you like to change?
kitchen: Name two or more things necessary to your *survival* that may be found in this room.	**backyard/park:** What sport could you play that uses *aggression* in a useful way?
your room: What is an *inborn* talent or trait that you have?	**family room:** Do you have a *propensity* for relaxing alone or relaxing with others?
front door: What do you do to increase *security* at night?	**bathroom:** What first-aid *resources* do you have on hand?
family room: When you've had a *devastating* experience, who comforts you?	**kitchen:** What do you do to *eradicate* germs in this room?

> I can be clumsy, and I have a <u>propensity</u> to fall. If my shoelaces come untied, it's <u>inevitable</u> that I'll trip over myself! My friends are <u>persistent</u> in making fun of me for this, but I laugh it off.

Master It: Use Words in Meaningful Ways

Survival Guide

Directions: In this activity, you'll write a survival guide suitable for students at your school. Work with a partner if your teacher approves, and follow these steps:

1. Choose a topic for your survival guide. For ideas, skim the vocabulary words. Words such as *security* and *aggression* may suggest a topic of school safety. Words such as *resources* and *persistent* could link to test taking. You should use at least *two* vocabulary words in your guide.

2. Write your survival guide, paying attention to format and tone.

   > *Format:* You may use a bullet list format, a "top ten" list, a paragraph format, or another format you choose.

   > *Tone:* You can make your guide humorous or serious, realistic or outlandish. The tone is up to you.

3. Read your survival guide aloud to a small group or the class.

Reading a Fiction Text

The following passage comes from a short story. As you read the passage, use context clues to try to figure out the meaning of the underlined words.

Group Work Gone Wrong

Kevin grimaced when he glanced at the calendar. "Tomorrow's the day," he groaned.

"What's wrong?" his father asked. "You look as dejected as a batter who's just made the last out of the game. Why the big frown?"

"It's this Spanish project for school. Three of us are supposed to work together to write a scene and then present it to the class. But I'm the only one who's memorized his lines."

"Why's that?"

"Why's that?" Kevin repeated, sounding exasperated. "I'll tell you why. Because Emily spends all her time text-messaging instead of concentrating on what we're doing, and Nicole has the attention span of a frog."

"I can understand your frustration. Have you expressed your annoyance to the girls?"

"Of course, and both of them always say they're sorry and act contrite. But a half hour later, Emily's back on her cell phone, and Nicole is spacing out again. Their remorse doesn't last very long."

"Maybe Nicole's mom could help. Isn't she a teacher?"

"Yeah, but she's more a hindrance than a help."

"What do you mean?"

"She keeps on suggesting modifications to the script, even after we tell her a hundred times that we're done making changes. It's pretty infuriating sometimes, but what can we do? She thinks she's helping, so we don't want to be insolent and snap at her."

"Do you want me to get involved? I'm not fluent in Spanish, but I know enough to get by."

"That's okay, Dad. But thanks. I'll handle it."

Write your definition of each word on the lines below. Then compare your definitions to those in List 22.

grimace _____

_____

dejected _____

_____

exasperate _____

_____

frustration _____

_____

contrite _____

_____

remorse _____

_____

hindrance _____

_____

modification _____

_____

insolent _____

_____

fluent _____

_____

List 22 Words from a Fiction Text

Read each word, what it means, and how it's used. Were your definitions correct?

Word	What It Means	How It's Used
grimace *(v, n)* GRI-muhs	to twist the face in an expression of displeasure or pain; frown	Elizabeth *grimaced* when she bumped her elbow against the table.

continued

dejected *(adj)* di-JEK-tid	unhappy; discouraged	William felt *dejected* after losing the chess match.
exasperate *(v)* ig-ZAS-puh-rate	to annoy or make angry; irritate	Megan has the *exasperating* habit of always arriving late for appointments.
frustration *(n)* fruhs-TRAY-shuhn	feeling of irritation or annoyance; aggravation	My *frustration* grew as I tried calling for twenty minutes but kept getting a busy signal.
contrite *(adj)* kuhn-TRITE	feeling or showing sorrow or regret; regretful	Feeling *contrite* for what he had done, Ethan apologized.
remorse *(n)* ri-MAWRS	regret for wrongdoing	The criminal felt no *remorse* for the crime he had committed.
hindrance *(n)* HIN-druhnts	something that hinders or gets in the way; obstacle	The curious kitten proved to be a *hindrance* when we tried to do a jigsaw puzzle.
modification *(n)* mah-duh-fuh-KAY-shuhn	a change; alteration or adjustment	The experimental engine did not perform as well as hoped, so scientists made several *modifications*.
insolent *(adj)* IN-suh-luhnt	boldly insulting, disrespectful, or rude	John's *insolent* behavior toward his classmates landed him in the principal's office.
fluent *(adj)* FLOO-uhnt	able to use a language easily and expressively	Having lived in Madrid for several years, Dan had become *fluent* in Spanish.

Own It: Develop Your Word Understanding

Follow the Clues

Directions: In this activity, you'll learn more about the value of—and possible shortfalls of—context clues. Follow these steps:

1. Scan the passage on page 149, noting the context clues that helped you determine the meanings of vocabulary words. Then, on a sheet of paper, list the words and the context clues. If you can't identify a context clue for a word, write "no context clue."

2. In a small group, discuss context clues. To get the conversation started, answer some of the questions in the box.

> For which underlined words did you find context clues?

> Did any underlined words seem to have no context clues? If so, which ones?

> Did people in your group come up with different definitions for the same word? Why do you think this happened?

> Did context clues seem to mislead you about the meanings of any words? If so, explain.

> When using context clues to determine a word's meaning, what can readers do to make sure this meaning is accurate?

Tip: Using a Dictionary

When you come across a word you don't know, and you are unable to figure out its meaning from context, you may need to look it up in a dictionary. But dictionaries often show different forms of a word and give more than one definition. How do you know which definition is the one you need? Here are some hints.

1. First, check the part of speech. For example, if the word in question is being used as a noun (the name of a person, place, thing, or idea), then look at the noun definitions.

2. Next, check the definitions given under that part of speech and see which one makes sense in the context of what you're reading.

Imagine you looked up *security* from the last paragraph of the nonfiction passage that begins on page 143. Which dictionary definition most accurately captures the meaning of *security* as used in the passage?

> **security** *n.* **1** the state of being secure—safe from danger or anxiety **2** something that is given to ensure the fulfillment of an obligation **3** a document that provides of ownership of an investment

The passage states that fires helped people feel more secure, and "Greater security enabled people to live longer, and the population increased." Security is used as a noun (as a concept) to describe the feeling that safe, positive people had. So the correct definition is "**1** the state of being secure—safe from danger or anxiety."

Link It: Make Word-to-World Connections

Person, Place, or Thing?

Directions: Follow these steps to complete the activity.

1. Read each word in the first column of the table below.

2. In the second column, complete the sentence by writing the name of a person, place, or thing.

3. In the third column, write a sentence or two explaining the connection. Try to use the key word in your explanation. A sample response for *grimace* is completed for you.

This word . . .	. . . makes me think of . . .	Sentence
grimace	Dad.	He always grimaces when I ask if I can have some money.
grimace		
dejected		
exasperate		
frustration		
remorse		
contrite		
hindrance		
modification		
insolent		
fluent		

Master It: Use Words in Meaningful Ways

What Happens Next?

Directions: Reread the portion of the story about Kevin on page 149. Based on what has happened so far, what do you think will happen next? Write an ending telling the next part of the story. Use as many of the vocabulary words as you can. Then participate in a storytelling festival during which you and classmates entertain one another with your tales.

Some helpful suggestions are included in the box below.

Your Narrative Process

> To get your ideas flowing, have a brainstorming session with classmates.

> In your story, focus on *one* event, problem, or solution.

> You can focus on dialogue (conversation between characters) or action—or a mix of both.

> Ask yourself, What would this character do? Think? Say?

> Share a draft of your story with a classmate. Get feedback about what is interesting and what is confusing.

> Practice reading your story aloud at home before you read it aloud in class.

Reading a Science Text

The following passage is from a science textbook. As you read the passage, use context clues to try to figure out the meaning of the underlined words.

Tropical Rain Forests

Tropical rain forests are located mainly along the equator. There are rain forests in the Amazon basin of South America, the land drained by the Amazon and its branches. There are also rain forests in the Congo region of Africa, the East Indies, and the southern tip of Florida.

The average temperature in a tropical rain forest is high and varies little from day to day. The yearly rainfall is 100 inches or more. The combination of high temperatures and daily rains results in high humidity, which favors the growth of rich, <u>luxuriant</u> vegetation. The lush plant life and tall, leafy trees create a true natural wonder. Most species of trees in the tropical rain forest retain their leaves all year. The dry season here corresponds to the winter season of the <u>temperate zone</u>, the area of the earth's surface between the tropics and the polar circles.

In the tropical rain forest, most of the <u>lofty</u> trees are broad-leaved and allow little sunlight to reach the forest floor. The soil lacks minerals because the daily rains dissolve and wash away, or <u>leach</u>, the mineral salts. This soil condition prevents small plants from growing on the forest floor. <u>Epiphytes</u>—plants that live on other plants—such as orchids, certain ferns, and Spanish moss, obtain their water from aerial roots or from cup-shaped leaves that catch and hold water. Few animals live on the forest floor. Most of them, such as monkeys, sloths, and reptiles, live in the trees. The <u>diversity</u> of insects and birds is amazing. In fact, a small part of a tropical rain forest contains more species than are found in all of Europe.

Tropical rain forests are remarkable not only for their variety of plant and animal inhabitants but also for the <u>intricate</u> way in which these inhabitants <u>interrelate</u>. Because of the complicated relationships among the rain forest plants and animals, the elimination of one species may cause certain others to die out.

Write your definition of each word on the lines below. Then compare your definitions to those in List 23.

tropical rain forest _____

_____

basin _____

_____

luxuriant _____

_____

temperate zone _____

_____

lofty _____

_____

leach _____

_____

epiphyte _____

_____

diversity _____

_____

intricate _____

_____

interrelate _____

_____

List 23   Words from a Science Text

Read each word, what it means, and how it's used. Were your definitions correct?

Word	What It Means	How It's Used
tropical rain forest _(n)_ TRAH-pi-kuhl rain FAWR-ist	a dense tropical woodland having a yearly rainfall of 100 inches or more and characterized by tall, broad-leaved evergreen trees and lush vegetation	Some species of animals and plants are found only in the world's _tropical rain forests._

continued

basin *(n)* BAY-suhn	the land drained by a river and its branches	The Mississippi River *basin* drains more than 40 percent of the continental United States.
luxuriant *(adj)* lug-ZHOOR-ee-uhnt	abundant; lush	The magnificent mansion was surrounded by *luxuriant* gardens.
temperate zone *(n)* TEM-per-it zone	the area of Earth's surface between the tropics and the polar circles	Japan and northern Europe are in the *temperate zone* of the northern hemisphere.
lofty *(adj)* LAWF-tee	very high	The *lofty* mountain peaks were covered with snow.
leach *(v)* leech	to dissolve and wash away	Heavy rains can *leach* minerals from soil.
epiphyte *(n)* EH-puh-fite	a plant that grows on another plant	Some *epiphytes*, such as orchids, attach themselves to trees.
diversity *(n)* di-VUR-si-tee	variety; mixture	Many people travel to Africa to see the *diversity* of wildlife.
intricate *(adj)* IN-tri-kit	complicated; complex	It requires concentration to solve an *intricate* problem.
interrelate *(v)* in-ter-ri-LATE	to be linked or mutually related	Historians study the way past events *interrelate*.

Own It: Develop Your Word Understanding

Sound Memories

Directions: A useful technique for learning new words is to use multiple *senses*. For instance, by reading the list of vocabulary words, you used your sense of sight. In this activity, you'll use your sense of hearing to further study the words. Here's what to do:

1. Form a group of five people. Assign two vocabulary words to each of you.

2. On your own, do two things for each of your words or terms:

   a. Divide the word into syllables. (A dictionary can help.)

   b. Practice saying the word aloud. Pay attention to which syllable is stressed. Make sure you *enunciate* precisely. Don't slur syllables together or drop a sound that should be spoken.

3. Regroup and take turns doing the following things.

a. Speak each of your words or terms aloud, enunciating carefully.

b. Pause after each word or term. Ask your listeners to write down the word/term, spelling it as they hear it. Ask them to mark stressed syllables with an accent mark.

4. Regroup with the entire class. Share insights and ask questions. Perhaps, before this activity, you pronounced *tropical* as "tropcal," leaving out the *i*. Or perhaps you discovered that some people pronounce *diversity* with a long-*i* sound, and some people pronounce it with a short-*i* sound.

In math, our teacher had us work out <u>intricate</u> problems with lots of <u>interrelated</u> data for homework. It took a substantial amount of my time, but I was diligent about it and actually got most of them right.

Link It: Make Word-to-World Connections

Making Sense

Directions: In the previous activity, you used your senses of sight and hearing to study vocabulary words. Now think of all five senses: sight, hearing, taste, touch, smell. Which sense(s) could you use to further explore a specific vocabulary word?

You could, for example, use *sight* and *touch* to use a globe to locate a *tropical rain forest* and a *temperate zone*. You could use *taste* and *smell* to evaluate a *diversity* of ethnic foods and identify your favorite.

Get the idea? Use your imagination to generate ideas for connecting vocabulary words and one (or more) senses. Then carry out *one* of your ideas. Finally, share the results with your class.

Master It: Use Words in Meaningful Ways

What Do YOU Think?

Directions: In this activity, you'll write a statement using a vocabulary word and then get responses to your statement from classmates. Here's how the activity works.

1. Skim the list of vocabulary words, letting them spark ideas in your mind. Write down a statement or opinion using one vocabulary word. (For example, "It makes me sad to think of how *tropical rain forests* are being destroyed.)

2. Mingle among your classmates, stopping to talk with different people. Read your statement, then ask, "What do YOU think?" Some people may agree with you, others may disagree, and others may point out a related idea.

3. In a class discussion, share your statement and some of the responses you got.

Reading a History Text

The following passage comes from a history textbook. As you read the passage, use context clues to try to figure out the meaning of the underlined words.

Studying the Past

The term *culture* refers to the way of life of a group of people. It includes that group's religion, values, language, customs, art, music, literature, technology, economic system, and political system. The scientific study of human cultures—both past and present—is called anthropology. Those who study anthropology are anthropologists.

Studying Cultures of the Past

What evidence do scholars look at when studying various cultures? Books, newspapers, and other written records help them to draw conclusions about historic cultures—those with a written record. But how can scholars learn about people of the distant past who had not yet invented a system of writing? Prehistoric cultures are those cultures of the past whose people did not leave any written record. Fortunately, however, prehistoric peoples left behind artifacts of their culture that can be examined and interpreted. Artifacts are human-made objects, ranging from pottery and tools to statues and pyramids. The social science that is most directly concerted with such evidence of past cultures is called archaeology, a branch of anthropology.

Sometimes archaeologists, those who study ancient artifacts, can directly view stone monuments or other structures that are still standing. More often, they must dig in the ground to find the remains of buildings, burial sites, and campsites. Each artifact that they find through their diligent work can become a clue to learning how a prehistoric people lived.

Archaeologists can determine the approximate age of bones and other artifacts in a burial site by a process called radiocarbon dating. Their instruments measure the amount of radioactive carbon that is present in an object. Since radioactive carbon slowly decays at a constant rate, the amount of it that remains in an artifact tells archaeologists approximately how old it is.

Another important clue to the prehistoric past is provided by oral traditions. In some societies that did not develop writing systems, knowledge of the past has been transmitted by word of mouth. Thus, the stories, folktales, songs, and poems of a people are often of ancient origin and provide substantial clues to the way their early ancestors lived. In many societies, traditional folktales and songs continue to have importance because they help maintain cultural identity, the characteristics that make a particular culture unique.

Write your definition of each word on the lines that follow. Then compare your definitions to those in List 24.

anthropology _____

_____

prehistoric _____

_____

artifact _____

_____

archaeologist _____

_____

diligent _____

_____

radiocarbon dating _____

_____

decay _____

_____

oral tradition _____

_____

substantial _____

_____

identity _____

_____

List 24   Words from a History Text

Read each word, what it means, and how it's used. Were your definitions correct?

Word	What It Means	How It's Used
anthropology _(n)_ an-thruh-PAH-luh-jee	the scientific study of human beings and their culture	Scientists who study _anthropology_ explore the relationships that exist within different social groups.

continued

prehistoric *(adj)* pree-his-TAWR-ik	before recorded history	Dinosaurs roamed Earth in *prehistoric* times.
artifact *(n)* AHR-tuh-fakt	a human-made object	The stone tool was an *artifact* from an ancient civilization.
archaeologist *(n)* ahr-kee-AH-luh-jist	a scientist who studies human life and activities of the past	The *archaeologist* discovered bones and teeth buried deep in the ground.
diligent *(adj)* DI-lih-juhnt	careful and steady; painstaking	Maria made a *diligent* search for her misplaced car key.
radiocarbon dating *(n)* ray-dee-oh-KAHR-buhn DAYT-ing	a method of determining the approximate age of an object by measuring the amount of radioactive carbon it contains	Using *radiocarbon dating*, scientists were able to estimate the age of the ancient fossil.
decay *(v)* di-KAY	(of a radioactive substance) to disintegrate or become less	Scientists know the rate at which radioactive carbon *decays*.
oral tradition *(n)* AWR-uhl tru-DIH-shuhn	the preservation and sharing of past knowledge through spoken communication	Ancient legends are passed on to future generations through *oral tradition*.
substantial *(adj)* suhb-STAN-shuhl	of a considerable or significant amount, quantity, or size	There are some *substantial* flaws in the building's structure that are going to take a long time to repair.
identity *(n)* eye-DEN-ti-tee	individuality; uniqueness	People's customs and traditions reflect their national *identity*.

Own It: Develop Your Word Understanding

Game Show

Directions: In this activity, you will be part of a game show team. When your team is "onstage" (in front of the class), the rest of the class will be your audience. They may clap, boo, or cheer as they watch. Here's how the game show works:

1. Assemble your team onstage. Choose one or two hosts, while the rest of you line up as contestants.

2. The host reads the definition of a vocabulary word. This is the *answer* to a question. If you know the *question*, raise your hand.

3. The host calls on the first person to raise a hand. This person must ask the *question* that matches the host's answer. For instance, if the host read, "A ruler of ancient Egypt," then the correct question is, "What is a pharaoh?"

4. Each correct *question* wins a point. The game is over when each definition has been matched to the correct question. Finally, add up contestants' points to see who won.

Link It: Make Word-to-World Connections

New Contexts

Directions: When you read the passage on pages 159–160, you read each vocabulary word in the context of the topic "studying cultures of the past." In this activity, you'll choose a vocabulary word and put it into a *different* context. Grab a partner and follow these steps:

1. Toss around ideas for how you could put vocabulary words into different contexts. For instance, you could use *prehistoric* in a description of a dinosaur. You could use *archaeologist* to tell about a movie, or use *oral tradition* to describe a special tradition in your family.

2. Based on your ideas in step 1, choose the word you would most like to work with. (You can each choose a different word and then help each other with step 3. Or you can both choose the same word and complete step 3 together.)

3. Use your creativity to bring the word to life in its new context. A basic plan, for instance, is to write a paragraph. For added appeal, use graphics, music, costumes, or objects along with your written or spoken words (this is when a partner comes in handy!).

4. Present your word in its new context to the class.

Master It: Use Words in Meaningful Ways

Did You Know?

Directions: In this activity, you will choose one vocabulary word to explore further. Then you'll share a few facts about this word with your classmates. Follow these steps:

1. Review the list of vocabulary words and their meanings. Choose a word that seems interesting to you.

2. Find *two or three* facts about the word that you can share with your class. For instance, who are some historical figures who used a secret *identity*? What does the business term "due *diligence*" mean? Useful sources of information include textbooks, encyclopedias, documentaries, knowledgeable people, and articles.

3. Write a few sentences stating two or three facts about the vocabulary word. Here are some phrases that you could use to begin the sentences.

> Did you know that . . .

> A surprising fact about (*vocabulary word*) is . . .

> A question I had about (*vocabulary word*) was . . .

4. Practice reading your sentences aloud. Then read your sentences to your classmates.

Wrapping Up: Review What You've Learned

Here's a brief summary of what you've studied in this chapter.

> When you encounter a word whose meaning you're not sure about, context clues can help you figure out the meaning of the word.

> **Context** is the words or sentences that precede and follow a particular word.

> Sometimes you need very little context to figure out a word's meaning. Other times, you may have to consider a whole paragraph.

> There are various kinds of context clues:

descriptive details

explanations or definitions

examples

synonyms and antonyms

comparison and contrast

> Combining your knowledge of word parts with your knowledge of context clues can make it easier to figure out the meaning of unfamiliar words.

Flaunt It: Show Your Word Understanding

In the following exercises, you'll demonstrate your understanding of each vocabulary word. You will use vocabulary words, or forms of the words, to complete sentences and to write sentences of your own.

A Sentence Completion

Directions: Circle the letter of the pair of words or terms that best complete each sentence.

1. The Amazon jungle is the biggest _____ in the world. Running like a snake through the warm, lush region is the Amazon River, which drains the Amazon _____.

   a. temperate zone, basin

   b. resource, epiphyte

   c. artifact, anthropology

   d. tropical rain forest, basin

2. After an argument with her sister, Zandra cut off some of the other girl's long, _____ hair while she slept. Later, upon seeing her sister's anguish, Zandra felt _____.

   a. luxuriant, contrite

   b. persistent, aggression

   c. luxuriant, diligent

   d. devastating, dejected

3. Frida's _____ to bicker unpleasantly with friends became her downfall. Her friends, feeling _____ with Frida's unpleasantness, quit spending time with her.

   a. oral tradition, decay

   b. propensity, frustration

   c. security, eradication

   d. persistence, grimace

4. My grandpa always told me, "When you hurry, mistakes are _____." Even though his "lessons" sometimes _____ me, I miss them now that he is no longer with us.

   a. inborn, leached

b. lofty, hindered

c. inevitable, exasperated

d. modification, survived

5. I dream of becoming an _____ so that I can study the ruins of ancient civilizations. Part of my job would be using _____ to determine how old some of the artifacts are.

   a. archaeologist, radiocarbon dating

   b. anthropology, identity

   c. archaeologist, diversity

   d. anthropology, eradication

B Word Bank

Directions: Choose a word from the box to complete each sentence. Write the word on the blank in the sentence. Each word may be used only once.

persistent	inborn	identity	propensity	inevitable
diversity	prehistoric	lofty	eradicated	archaeologists

As a child, I became fascinated with the **(6)**_____ world. At first, I focused all my attention on dinosaurs. I knew the **(7)**_____ of each dinosaur that **(8)**_____ had discovered and reconstructed. My curiosity made me **(9)**_____, and I read every book in the kids' section of the library that could tell me about that era of Earth's history. I wondered, what had **(10)**_____ the dinosaurs from the world? Could such destruction ever happen again?

It was **(11)**_____ that my interests would move beyond dinosaurs. I began to wonder about the earth's landscape. When had the **(12)**_____ mountains formed? Before the mountains, was the landscape flat? How had **(13)**_____ among plants and animals developed? I've always had a **(14)** _____ to ask a lot of questions!

Eventually, my **(15)**_____ curiosity led me to become a history professor. You can probably guess what the focus of my teaching and research is.

C Writing

Directions: Follow the directions to write sentences using vocabulary words. Write your sentences on a separate sheet of paper.

16. Use *exasperate* in a sentence about a friend.

17. Use *resources* in a sentence about a library.

18. Use *fluent* and *diligent* in the same sentence.

19. Use *aggression* and *hindrance* in the same sentence.

20. Use *grimace* and *frustration* in the same sentence.

Chapter Extension Activities

Activities à la Carte: Extend Your Word Knowledge

The activities on this page are presented à la carte, like items on a restaurant menu, meaning that you can choose from a variety of options. Your teacher may assign an activity or let you pick the one that tempts your appetite. If time allows, you might do more than one activity. All of the activities feature the same ingredient: **context clues**. Dig in!

Curious George

Did a vocabulary word or reading topic in this chapter pique your curiosity? Learn more about it by designing your own research project. Your final product could be written, painted, programmed on a computer, filmed, or created in some other way. Include a glossary of key words and their definitions. Share your project with your teacher and with someone else who shares your curiosity.

My Own Personal Context

How does social context influence your word choices? For a week, be aware of how you talk in different situations—in a class, at a party, at a religious meeting, with a friend, with an enemy, and so on. Each day, record social contexts and key words that you used in each context. After a week, evaluate your lists and draw conclusions. Do you use the same vocabulary in all social situations? Or do your word choices vary based on context?

Eavesdrop

Context clues can be a valuable tool in deductive reasoning. In this type of reasoning, you take general information and draw a specific conclusion from it. To try it out, eavesdrop on strangers' conversations. In a notebook, jot down odd bits of the discussions you overhear. Using clues in what you wrote, make educated guesses about what the full conversations were about. Share some interesting results with your class.

Sling Some Slang

Many slang words carry meaning based on how they are used in a sentence—based on context, in other words. Brainstorm a list of slang words and terms that you and your friends use. Choose five of them that could have different meanings depending on how they are used. Then write sentences showing at least two uses of each word or term.

It's Greek to Me

If you have studied a second language, then you know what it's like to struggle to translate a sentence. You start with words you know and use those words as clues to the meanings of unfamiliar words. With a language-study group or your class, share some examples of how you learned new foreign words using context clues.

Track Five

For the next five days, keep track of new words you learn by studying context clues. Try to collect examples from all types of reading that you do—school assignments, magazines, fiction, messages from friends, and so on. After five days, you'll have a concrete measure of how much your literacy has increased.

The Survey Says . . .

Survey students about vocabulary and/or reading habits, and prepare charts or graphs of the results. First, develop three to five survey questions, such as "Do you plan to remember key words learned at school?" or "How often do you read for pleasure: once a day, once a week, once a month, or never?" Survey a sampling of students. Then create data sheets showing the results. Report to your classmates—they may be surprised at what the numbers suggest.

Clue Review

Using context clues to determine word meaning can serve you well long after this lesson is over. With this in mind, create a poster-sized cheat sheet that lists and explains the types of context clues taught in this lesson. Use colorful paint or paper to make the poster eye-catching. Hang this clue review in your classroom or near a table where you normally do homework.

Thinking About Different Word Meanings

8

In a sense, words are like tools. As a writer, you choose the right tools to do the job. As a reader, you respond to how authors use words to create meaning. With experience in reading and writing, you gain greater skill in using the tools of the trade: words.

This chapter offers you three types of tools to add to your toolbox. You'll learn about words with more than one meaning, literal and figurative uses of words, and descriptive words with precise meanings. Chances are, you'll recognize some of these words. Others will be new discoveries.

Sneak Peek: Preview the Lesson

Tools of the Trade

Take a look at some of the words you'll learn in this chapter. Which ones are familiar? Which ones are new to you? Which words seem so "foreign" that you can't imagine ever using them? On the next page, sort the words into categories, based on your responses. (You can put a word in more than one category.) After you complete the lesson, come back to this activity and evaluate your progress in adding "tools" to your vocabulary toolbox!

Word List

accessory	probe	pummel	drastic	attentive
circuit	reproduce	blemish	juvenile	energetic
dictate	tragedy	sparse	singular	jovial

I've seen this word before.	I've used this word before.	I have not used this word.	I can't imagine ever using this word.

Vocabulary Mini-Lesson: Understanding Words with More than One Meaning

When you look up a word in a dictionary, you often find that the word has more than one meaning. Consider the word *scale*, for example. How many meanings of this word can you think of? Compare the following sentences.

The nurse weighed the patient on the <u>scale</u>.

The body of this fish is covered with <u>scales</u>.

The <u>scale</u> of this map is one inch to 50 miles.

Ben practiced the trumpet until he could hit the highest note on the <u>scale</u>.

And these are just some of the *noun* meanings! There are other noun meanings, too, as well as several *verb* meanings.

While most words don't have as many meanings as *scale* does, you may be surprised by how many words do have more than one meaning. You may also be surprised to find that many familiar words have less familiar additional meanings. For example, when you hear the word *jet*, you no doubt think of airplanes or engines. But did you know that jet is also a kind of coal?

Words to Know: Vocabulary Lists and Activities

In this section, you'll study two lists of words with more than one definition.

List 25   Words with Multiple Meanings

Read each word, its two or three different meanings, and how it's used. Are any of the definitions surprising to you?

Word	What It Means	How It's Used
accessory *(n)* ik-SEH-suh-ree	1. something of secondary importance that adds to an object's usefulness, appearance, or comfort	1. Headsets and car chargers are useful *accessories* for a cell phone.
	2. a person who assists in or contributes to a crime	2. The man's failure to report the crime makes him an *accessory*.
application *(n)* a-pli-KAY-shuhn	1. act or manner of applying or using	1. This is a challenging task that requires the *application* of many skills.
	2. relevance; connection	2. The lawyer argued that the witness's testimony had no *application* to the case.
	3. a request, or the form used to make a request	3. Jonathan filled out an *application* for a summer job.
bearing *(n)* BAIR-ing	1. manner of carrying oneself; behavior	1. Even as a child, the prince already had a regal *bearing*.
	2. relation; connection; relevance	2. The student's comment has little *bearing* on the topic.
circuit *(n)* SUR-kit	1. the act of moving around; circular passage	1. Earth completes its *circuit* of the sun in one year.
	2. the complete path by which an electric current flows	2. Flipping the switch closes the *circuit* and turns on the light.

continued

| depression *(n)*
di-PREH-shuhn | **1.** an emotional condition characterized by such feelings as sadness and hopelessness | **1.** People who suffer from *depression* should seek help from a mental health professional. |
| | **2.** a low or sunken place in a surface | **2.** It was a bumpy car ride because of the many *depressions* in the old dirt road. |

Own It: Develop Your Word Understanding

Multiple-Meaning Mixer

Directions: In this activity, you will be given a vocabulary word *or* a definition. Your job is to find a classmate who has the corresponding vocabulary word or definition. Here's how the activity works:

1. Your teacher will write the vocabulary words and definitions on index cards, then put the cards in a box.
2. You take one card from the box.
3. Move around the classroom to find the person who has the word or definition that corresponds to what's written on your card. Since each word has more than one meaning, you'll form a group of three or four people.
4. With your group, review the multiple meanings of your word. Practice explaining the word's meanings in your own words rather than repeating the definitions in the book. Then write sentences that demonstrate the different meanings.
5. In a class discussion, take turns with members of your group to explain your word's multiple meanings and read your sentences aloud.

Link It: Make Word-to-World Connections

Me, Myself, and I

Directions: In this activity, you'll choose *one* meaning of each vocabulary word to use in a description of yourself or your world. Follow these steps:

1. The vocabulary words are listed in the following table. Decide which meaning of each word best connects to your life—to an experience you've had, for instance, or to a description of yourself or your community.

2. In the space beside each key word, explain which meaning of the word best connects to your life and why.

3. Share some of your results with the class.

Key Word	Meaning That Best Connects to Me and My World
accessory	
application	
bearing	
circuit	
depression	

Master It: Use Words in Meaningful Ways

Wanted: YOU!

Directions: Skim the following classified advertisements. Choose one that interests you and write a reply. You can be creative with your details and can make up information as needed. In your reply, be sure to use the italicized vocabulary word.

Finally, read your reply aloud in a small group. Explain whether you would answer a similar classified ad in real life.

Old Firehouse Teen Center

Classifieds

Reply to ads by submitting responses to Teen Center, Director's Office.

Selling: Printer, scanner, and other PC *accessories*, cheap! They are used but work great. Will consider trades.	**Seeking:** Coaching assistants for community center sports program. Must enjoy working with young kids. Submit *application* ASAP.	**Announcing:** Support group for teens dealing with *depression* in self or family member. Meets twice a month at Teen Center. Led by licensed counselor.
Needed: Workout partner for *circuit* training 3 × per week. Must be reliable, dedicated. I am 14, male. Seeking male or female, close in age.	**Available:** Former model available for coaching in makeup *application*, professional bearing, and fashion style. Sessions take place at Teen Center.	**Wanted:** Volunteers to resurface football field by filling *depressions* with dirt. Play a game of flag football afterward. Food and drinks provided.
Reward: For information on burglary of Teen Center Food Bank. Thief wore letterman's jacket. *Accessory* knew security codes.	**Welcome:** Join our Poetry Slam! Current writing topic: Does money have any *bearing* on your happiness? Meets first Tuesday of month, 4:30 P.M.	**Wanted:** Volunteers for Pet Visit Program in local nursing home. Pets can help with *depression* felt by shut-ins. Bring your gentle pet, or work with ours!

List 26 Words with Multiple Meanings

Here is a second list of words with multiple definitions. Read each word, its two or three different meanings, and how it's used. Once again, see if any of the definitions are surprising to you.

Word	What It Means	How It's Used
dictate *(v)* DIK-tate	**1.** to say or impose with authority **2.** to speak or read (something) aloud for a person or machine to record	**1.** When the war ended, the victorious nation *dictated* the terms of peace. **2.** Foreign-language teachers often *dictate* passages to their students.
internal *(adj)* in-TUR-nuhl	**1.** relating to the inside **2.** relating to or occurring within an organization or nation	**1.** The accident victim suffered *internal* injuries to her liver. **2.** The conflict began when one country interfered in the *internal* affairs of another.
probe *(n)* prohb	**1.** a slender medical instrument used to explore a wound **2.** an investigation **3.** a spacecraft designed to explore and gather information about the atmosphere, outer space, or a planet	**1.** The dentist touched my tooth with a *probe*. **2.** A congressional committee launched a *probe* into possible illegal activities. **3.** The *probe* discovered evidence of water on Mars.
redeem *(v)* ri-DEEM	**1.** to take action to make up for wrongdoing; make amends for past deeds **2.** to turn in for something of value	**1.** Regretting what he'd done, Brandon was determined to *redeem* himself by helping people in need. **2.** You can *redeem* this coupon for a free beverage with your meal.
reproduce *(v)* ree-pruh-DOOS	**1.** to make a copy of **2.** to produce (new individuals of the same kind) by sexual or asexual means	**1.** We used a copy machine to *reproduce* the drawing. **2.** Nature has conceived clever ways for plants to *reproduce*.

Own It: Develop Your Word Understanding

A Few Questions

Directions: Work with a partner to complete the activity. For each numbered item, answer the question in the first column of the table.

Then, in the second column, write your own definition of the key word. Finally, in a class discussion, share some of your responses.

Question	My Definition of the Key Word, Based on Its Use in the Question
1. Besides yourself, who sometimes *dictates* what you can wear?	**dictate**
2. When doing homework, what is one thing you might *dictate* to a study buddy?	**dictate**
3. Name one of your *internal* organs.	**internal**
4. What is a tradition that is *internal* to your school?	**internal**
5. What is one reason why a dentist might use a *probe*?	**probe**
6. What is one reason why school officials might launch a *probe*?	**probe**
7. What is one reason why NASA might launch a space *probe*?	**probe**

continued

8. If you betray a friend, is it possible to *redeem* yourself?	**redeem**
9. Would you rather *redeem* a coupon for free pizza or free chocolate?	**redeem**
10. What is one thing that you have *reproduced* on a copy machine?	**reproduce**
11. Should pets be spayed/neutered, or allowed to *reproduce*?	**reproduce**

Link It: Make Word-to-World Connections

Give It a Week

Directions: For a week, watch for ways the vocabulary words relate to your world. Keep a notebook handy and jot down every idea, day by day. For instance, you may read a news story that mentions a police department's *internal* affairs division. You might have a discussion with a parent about rules *dictated* to you, or you might *redeem* a coupon.

Report back to your class. Tell how many examples you collected and read a few aloud. Tell whether you noticed examples for every word, or if a word didn't show up in your world that week. Some vocabulary words have more meanings than are listed in the table. If you used one of these additional meanings, be sure to point that out.

Master It: Use Words in Meaningful Ways

Letter to the Editor

Directions: Use a vocabulary word to inspire a letter to the editor of your school or local newspaper. A *letter to the editor* expresses the writer's personal opinions on a topic (often a controversial topic). To get your ideas flowing, think about these statements:

> ❯ A school should not be allowed to *dictate* a student dress code.
> ❯ Every pet has the right to *reproduce.*
> ❯ School employees should be allowed to carry out *probes* into students' personal lives.

For your letter, use one of these topics or another topic that you develop.

After you write your letter to the editor, your teacher will collect it in a folder with other students' letters. When you have a spare moment in class, pull out someone's letter and read it.

Vocabulary Mini-Lesson: Understanding Literal and Figurative Uses of Words

Most of the time, we use words according to their *literal* meaning, or dictionary definition. However, we can also use words *figuratively.* When you read figurative language, you must *interpret* the meaning instead of just defining the words. With figurative language, a writer creates a striking mental image or makes an idea memorable. Look at these examples.

Literal:	Michael has been taking drum lessons for a <u>year</u>.
	(Michael has literally been taking lessons for one year.)
Figurative:	"It will take me a <u>year</u> to write this research report!" Lisa said.
	(It won't actually take Lisa a year to write the report. It just seems that way, because there's so much work involved.)

When you use a word literally, you mean exactly what you say. When you use a word figuratively, you are expressing an idea creatively, not literally.

Here is another example of literal and figurative uses of a word.

Literal:	I <u>fried</u> two eggs in the pan.
	(The eggs were cooked over heat.)
Figurative:	It was so hot on the beach, my brain was <u>fried</u>!
	(The speaker is imaginatively conveying the idea of intense heat.)

When you read sentences that use words figuratively, remember this: The writer is expressing an idea creatively. You must interpret the figurative language in order to understand the word's use in the sentence. The following table will help you recognize ways words are used figuratively.

Type of Figurative Language	Explanation	Example
metaphor MEH-tuh-fore	a comparison of two things that says one thing *is* the other thing	It's time we bought a new computer. This one's a <u>dinosaur</u>.
simile SI-muh-lee	a comparison that uses a word such as *like* or *as*	Your room is so messy, it looks <u>like</u> the city dump!
hyperbole high-PUR-buh-lee	exaggeration to create an effect or to make a point	I received about a <u>million</u> text messages last night.

continued

personification	giving human qualities,	My too tight jeans are <u>urging</u> me to
per-sah-nuh-fi-KAY-shuhn	such as thoughts or speech, to animals or nonliving things	get more exercise.
irony	a statement of the	Pickles and chocolate—what a
EYE-ruh-nee	opposite of what is meant, often humorous	<u>delicious</u> combination!

When you see words used figuratively, as in the examples above, ask, "What image is the writer creating with this word?" or "What point is the writer making with this word?" These questions will help you understand the figurative use of a word.

Words to Know: Vocabulary Lists and Activities

List 27   Words Used Literally and Figuratively

Read each word, what it means, and how it's used literally and figuratively. Note the type of figurative language used in each example.

Word	What It Means	How It's Used
anesthetic *(n)* a-nuhs-THEH-tik	a substance, such as a drug, that causes an insensitivity to pain	*Literal:* Just before the surgery, an *anesthetic* was administered to the patient. *Metaphor:* For me, chocolate is an *anesthetic*. (Chocolate does not actually stop the sensation of pain. Calling it an anesthetic suggests that it helps the speaker feel better in painful situations.)
inaccessible *(adj)* in-ik-SEH-suh-buhl	not capable of being reached or entered	*Literal:* During the winter months, heavy snow makes the mountain village *inaccessible*. *Simile:* The president of the company is as *inaccessible* to reporters as an eagle in a nest. (The comparison to "an eagle in a nest" suggests that the president is all but impossible for reporters to reach.)

continued

tragedy *(n)* TRA-juh-dee	a disastrous or very sad event	*Literal:* The earthquake was a *tragedy* that claimed many lives. *Hyperbole:* Johanna considered the store's running out of chocolate ice cream to be a real *tragedy*. (No chocolate ice cream may make Johanna sad, but it's quite an exaggeration to call it a tragedy.)
pummel *(v)* PUH-muhl	to pound or beat, usually used in reference to fists	*Literal:* The boxer *pummeled* his opponent. *Personification:* Your angry looks *pummel* my heart. (A look cannot physically hit something, nor does a look have actual fists. The sentence suggests that the angry looks are emotionally painful to endure.)
accommodating *(adj)* uh-KAH-muh-day-ting	willing to please; obliging; helpful	*Literal:* The restaurant was very *accommodating*, giving us a large table by the window. *Irony:* How *accommodating* of you to offer to wash the dishes when there are only two plates to be done! (The speaker is using irony to point out that the offer to wash dishes is not very meaningful.)

Own It: Develop Your Word Understanding

Divide and Conquer

Directions: Work with a partner to complete the activity. Here's what to do.

1. Divide the ten sentences between you.
2. Read each of your sentences and decide if the underlined word is used literally or figuratively. Write *L* or *F* next to the sentence to indicate your answer.
3. Share your results with your partner and explain your answers.
4. In a class discussion, talk about sentences that were challenging or confusing. Revise your answers as necessary.

_____ 1. Tumbling down the drain, the ring became underline{inaccessible}.

_____ **2.** In a newspaper article, the journalist <u>pummeled</u> the mayor.

_____ **3.** Music is my <u>anesthetic</u>.

_____ **4.** The fire in the museum was a <u>tragedy</u>.

_____ **5.** My sister was truly <u>accommodating</u>, offering me the broken chair.

_____ **6.** That outfit is a <u>tragedy</u>.

_____ **7.** Your love is as <u>inaccessible</u> as the moon to me.

_____ **8.** The school cafeteria is <u>accommodating</u> to students' backgrounds, offering food from many different countries.

_____ **9.** DuJuan received an <u>anesthetic</u> before the dentist performed the root canal.

_____ **10.** Angry bystanders <u>pummeled</u> the mugger.

Link It: Make Word-to-World Connections

Trading Cards

Directions: In this activity, you'll use vocabulary words to create trading cards. Here's what to do.

1. Gather supplies. You'll need five index cards, pens, paints, photos, and any other art supplies you want to use.

2. On each card, print one vocabulary word.

3. On each card, draw or glue an image that corresponds to a use of the word. The use can be figurative or literal. For instance, on the *pummel* card, you could paste or draw a picture of something that pummels you figuratively, such as the hot sun, your debate opponent, or a basketball. Be sure to sign your name somewhere on each card!

4. In class, take part in a Trading Card Festival. Move around the room, showing your cards to classmates. Interpret your cards for others, or let them make their own interpretations. Trade your cards for other cards that capture your interest.

5. Keep your trading cards handy to use in the next activity.

Master It: Use Words in Meaningful Ways

Literal or Figurative?

Directions: In this activity, you'll practice using words literally and figuratively. Follow these steps.

1. Get out your five trading cards from the activity on page 184. Then form a small group with classmates.

2. Take turns holding up a card and stating one sentence to interpret the card. Be sure to use the vocabulary word in your sentence. Then pause and let others state whether you used the word literally or figuratively.

3. People may disagree about whether a word is used figuratively or literally. Stop and explore the possibilities, trying to come to an agreement.

4. In a class discussion, share some of your group's most interesting and challenging sentences.

List 28 — Words Used Literally and Figuratively

Read each word, what it means, and how it's used literally and figuratively. Note the type of figurative language used in each example.

Word	What It Means	How It's Used
blemish *(n)* BLEH-mish	a mark, spot, or flaw that detracts from the appearance	*Literal:* Samantha used makeup to cover a *blemish* on her cheek. *Metaphor:* The accusation left a *blemish* on Sean's reputation. (The figurative spot on Sean's reputation is being compared to a physical mark.)
sparse *(adj)* spahrs	few and scattered; thinly spread	*Literal:* Settlements are *sparse* along the frontier. *Simile:* Late at night, people on the street in this part of town are as *sparse* as beachgoers in winter. (The comparison to "beachgoers in winter" suggests that the streets are deserted.)
annihilate *(v)* uh-NIE-uh-late	to destroy completely	*Literal:* The powerful bomb *annihilated* several villages. *Hyperbole:* Our football team *annihilated* the opposing team 63–0.

continued

		(The team didn't actually destroy anyone, but *annihilate* suggests just how huge their victory was.)
lament *(v)* luh-MENT	to feel sorrow or regret; mourn	*Literal:* The people *lamented* the death of their queen. *Personification:* A chill wind howled through the canyon, *lamenting* summer's end. (The wind cannot actually express emotions.)
plausible *(adj)* PLAW-zuh-buhl	reasonable; believable	*Literal:* Given the available facts, the investigator's explanation of the fire's cause seems *plausible*. *Irony:* Your account of how the window was broken is so *plausible* it makes me laugh. (The speaker is using irony to indicate that the account is not really plausible at all.)

Own It: Develop Your Word Understanding

Two Sides of the Coin

Directions: Each vocabulary word is like a coin with two sides—a literal side and a figurative side. You have one coin but more than one way to "spend" it. To become familiar with literal and figurative uses of each word, complete the graphic organizers on the next two pages. Follow these steps:

1. On the **Literal** side of the coin, write a sentence that uses the word literally. For example, *Megan's sparse freckles are cute.*

2. On the **Figurative** side of the coin, write a sentence that uses the word figuratively. For example, *On my report card, A's are as sparse as whiskers on a baby.*

3. In a class discussion, share some of your work.

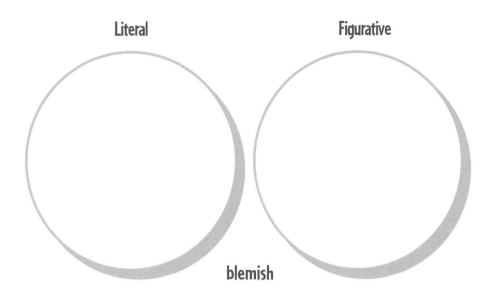

blemish

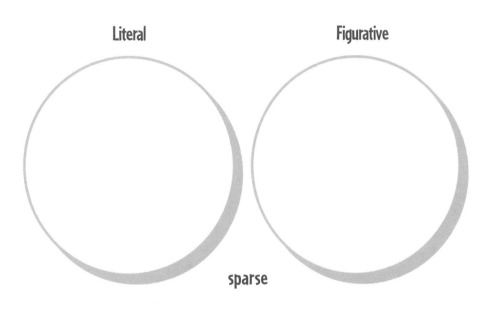

sparse

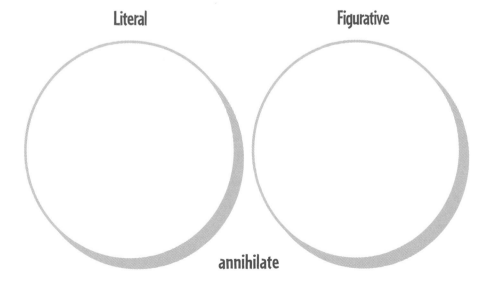

annihilate

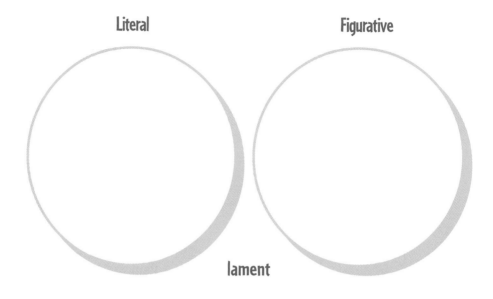

Literal   Figurative

lament

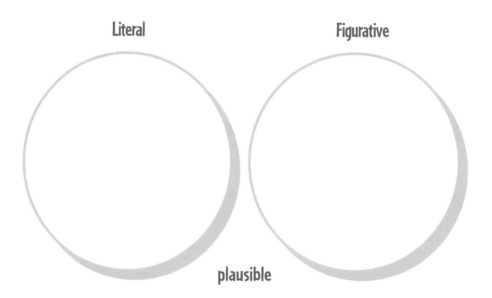

Literal   Figurative

plausible

Link It: Make Word-to-World Connections

Spin the Bottle

Directions: In this activity, you'll practice using words literally and figuratively. First, your teacher will place you in small groups and give each group an empty plastic bottle. Then follow these steps:

1. Appoint one person to be scribe for your group. This person writes down some of the sentences you create.

2. Place the bottle on a desk in the center of your group. One of you spins the bottle. When the bottle stops, ask the person it

points to, "Literal or figurative?" When the person chooses, give him or her a vocabulary word.

3. The person must make up a sentence that uses the vocabulary word literally or figuratively, depending on the choice made.

4. This person becomes the new bottle spinner, and the process repeats. If you run out of vocabulary words, use words from List 27 (pages 182–183).

5. In a class discussion, share some of your group's best and funniest sentences.

Master It: Use Words in Meaningful Ways

Five-Minute Mastery

Directions: In this activity, you'll write very quickly for five minutes about *one* vocabulary word. Here's how the activity works:

1. Choose one vocabulary word for this activity.

2. Get out a sheet of paper and set a timer for five minutes. (Your teacher may watch the time for you.) Begin by writing the first thought in your head about the vocabulary word. This thought could be a definition, a sentence using the word, a memory inspired by the word, or any other thought. There is no "wrong" thing to write.

3. Keep writing. Don't stop! Use the word literally. Use it figuratively. Write questions, lines of poetry, descriptions, statements, phrases, and anything else that comes to mind. Let one thought lead into the next.

4. After five minutes, stop writing.

5. Read what you wrote. Indulge in feelings of satisfaction and pride in your five-minute mastery of the vocabulary word.

Vocabulary Mini-Lesson: Using Descriptive Words with Specific Meanings

As writers and speakers, we're always using words to describe people, places, and things. For example:

Mrs. Burns is a nice neighbor.

We saw a great show at the Plymouth Playhouse.

The new restaurant in town is terrible.

However, when you hear descriptions like these, the best you can do is guess at their meaning.

What makes Mrs. Burns a "nice" neighbor? Is she thoughtful? Friendly? Helpful?

What made it a "great" show? Was it amusing? Exciting? Was the acting impressive?

In what way is the new restaurant "terrible"? Was the service poor? The food? The atmosphere?

Describing words like *nice*, *great*, and *terrible* give only a general idea of meaning. They are not precise (exact). By using specific descriptive words when you write and speak, you can convey your ideas more clearly.

Words to Know: Vocabulary Lists and Activities

The first list in this section contains words that describe behavior and actions, and the second list contains words that describe personality, character, and mood. Think about how these words create very specific images or ideas in your mind.

List 29 Words That Describe Behavior and Actions

These are words (adjectives) you'd use to describe the behavior or action of a person in your own life or of a character in a book or show. Read each word, what it means, and how it's used.

Word	What It Means	How It's Used
delirious *(adj)* di-LEER-ee-uhs	in a state of excited confusion	High fever made the patient *delirious*, causing him to see things that weren't there.
drastic *(adj)* DRAS-tik	strong or violent in effect; severe; extreme	Declaring war on another country is a *drastic* action to take.
haphazard *(adj)* hap-HAZ-erd	without a plan; random	The *haphazard* planting of flowers gave the garden a disorderly though colorful appearance.
hilarious *(adj)* hi-LAIR-ee-uhs	very funny; uproarious	The clown's *hilarious* performance made all the children laugh.

continued

juvenile *(adj)* JOO-vuh-nile	childish; immature	Joey's *juvenile* prank earned him a detention.
pathetic *(adj)* puh-THEH-tik	so unsuccessful or inadequate as to be pitiful	Rachel's *pathetic* attempt at humor made everyone groan.
quizzical *(adj)* KWIH-zi-kuhl	questioning; puzzled	Your *quizzical* expression suggests that you either don't understand what I said or you don't believe it.
ruthless *(adj)* ROOTH-lis	unfeeling; cruel; merciless	Ryan was *ruthless* in his pursuit of the prize, showing no regard for the feelings of others.
singular *(adj)* SING-gyuh-ler	exceptional; remarkable	Thomas Alva Edison is known for his *singular* achievements as an inventor.
steadfast *(adj)* STED-fast	firm in belief; unwavering; loyal	Campaign workers remained *steadfast* in their support, even though their candidate was trailing in the polls.

Own It: Develop Your Word Understanding

Box It

Directions: Fill in the boxes that surround each vocabulary word. List synonyms and antonyms of the key word, and list nouns that the key word could describe. Finally, sketch or write a memory cue to help you remember the word's meaning. (If your teacher approves, work with a partner to complete the activity.)

synonyms	nouns it could describe
delirious	
antonyms	memory cue

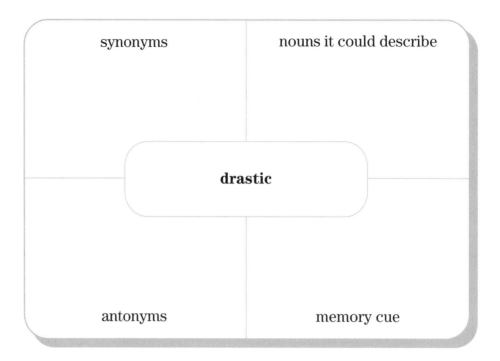

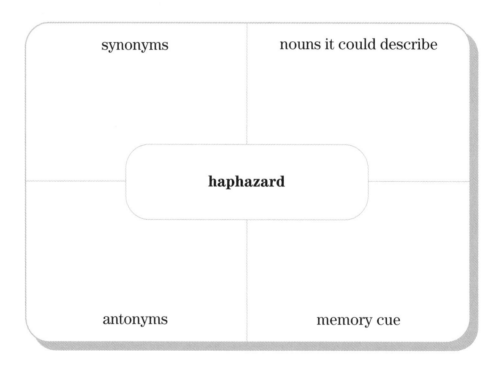

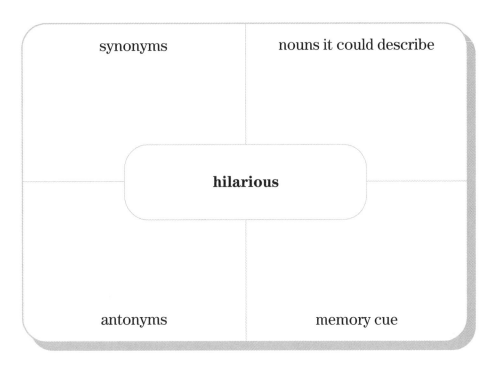

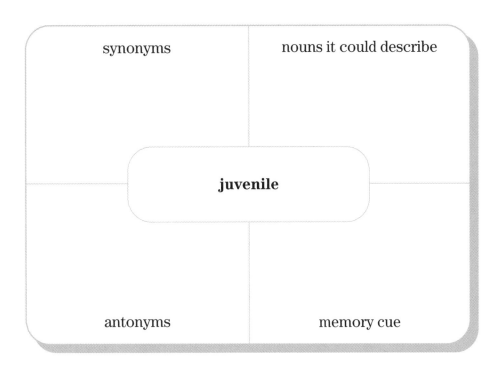

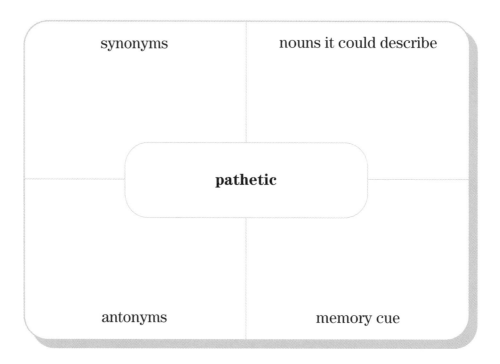

synonyms

nouns it could describe

pathetic

antonyms

memory cue

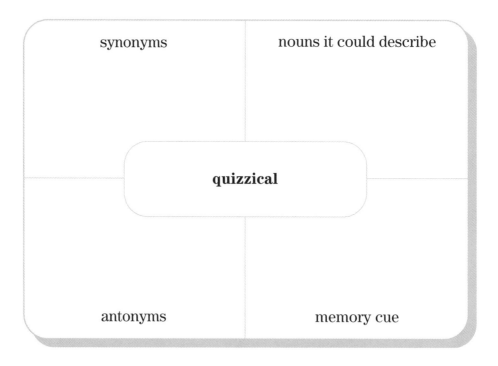

synonyms

nouns it could describe

quizzical

antonyms

memory cue

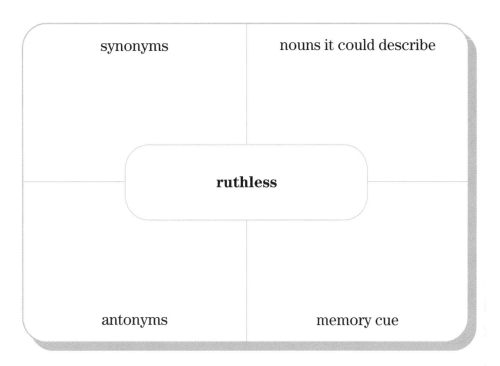

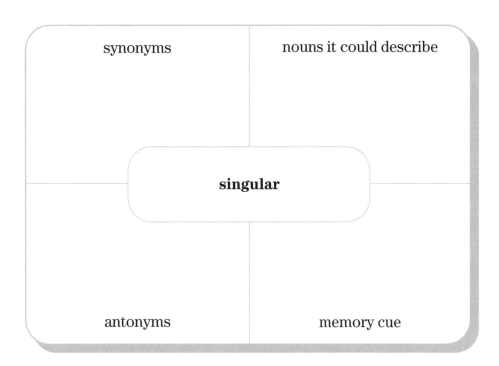

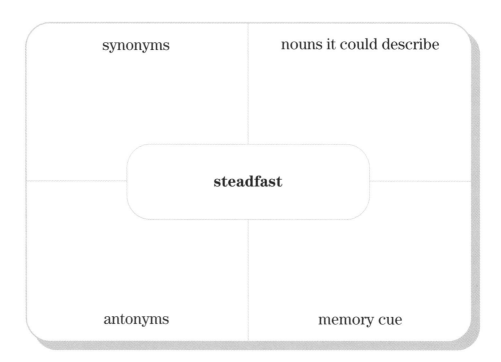

synonyms	nouns it could describe
steadfast	
antonyms	memory cue

Link It: Make Word-to-World Connections

I'm Thinking of a Word . . .

Directions: In this activity, you and your classmates will use the vocabulary words to describe things in your own lives. Here's how the activity works.

1. Cut two strips of paper. On each one, write the name of something in your life that could be described by one of the vocabulary words. For instance, you might write *weekend plans* on one slip and *ex-best friend* on the other.

2. Your teacher will collect all the slips of paper and jumble them in a box. Then he or she will take out one slip and read the word aloud.

3. Students suggest one or more vocabulary words that logically describe the word. (If the word is one of *your* two words, stay silent until others have had a chance to answer.)

4. Repeat the process with the next slip of paper from the box.

Master It: Use Words in Meaningful Ways

Passion Club

Directions: What is your passion? Do you love motorcycles or skateboarding or singing? Maybe you are passionate about nature or fashion or softball. In this activity, you'll choose something that you're passionate about and plan a club based on this passion. Here's what to do:

1. Brainstorm a list of all the things you really like—things you're passionate about.

2. Choose one passion that some of your friends would enjoy sharing with you.

3. Plan a "passion club" based on this interest. To plan the club, think about some of these questions: What is the purpose of the club? Who can join? How often will the club meet? What will you do at club meetings? What is the club's name?

4. Create a flyer that announces your club and gives details about it. On the flyer, use some of the vocabulary words, or forms of the words.

5. You can choose to hand out the flyer to your friends, or show it only to your teacher.

List 30 Words That Describe Personality, Character, or Mood

As you study these words, think of your own examples for how you'd use them to describe someone you know (real or fictional). Read each word, what it means, and how it's used.

Word	What It Means	How It's Used
amiable *(adj)* AY-mee-uh-buhl	friendly; good-natured	Zach is an *amiable* young man who gets along with everyone.
ardent *(adj)* AHR-dnt	passionate; enthusiastic	Evan is an *ardent* supporter of equal rights.
attentive *(adj)* uh-TEN-tiv	paying attention to the needs of others; considerate	We gave the waitress a generous tip because she was especially *attentive*.
elated *(adj)* i-LATE-id	in high spirits; delighted; overjoyed	Rebecca was *elated* to hear that she had won a prize in the art show.
energetic *(adj)* eh-ner-JE-tik	full of or showing energy; lively	The *energetic* new employee was the first one to arrive in the morning and the last to leave.
euphoric *(adj)* yoo-FAWR-ik	having strong or exaggerated feelings of happiness or well-being	Maria was *euphoric* when she got to shake hands with her celebrity crush.
haughty *(adj)* HAW-tee	having too much pride in oneself and disdain for others	The *haughty* queen refused to listen to her royal advisers, convinced that she knew best.
notorious *(adj)* noh-TAWR-ee-uhs	widely known and talked about, especially unfavorably	Police circulated a photo of the *notorious* bank robber.
resourceful *(adj)* ri-SAWRS-fuhl	able to handle challenges creatively and effectively	Tyler was *resourceful* enough to get himself out of the difficult situation.
sinister *(adj)* SI-nuhs-ter	wicked; evil	In the movie, the *sinister* villain steals the treasure map.

Own It: Develop Your Word Understanding

Accept or Reject?

Directions: In this activity, you'll spot fake definitions of the vocabulary words. Here's how the activity works:

1. Your teacher will assign you and a partner one of the vocabulary words. On an index card, write your names and the word you received. On the back of the card, write two things: a *correct* definition of the word and an *incorrect* definition that you make up. (Label each definition.) Make sure that your incorrect definition is still related to the correct one so that the wrong answer is not too obvious.

2. Your teacher will mix everyone's cards together in a box.

3. Your teacher will take out a card and read the vocabulary word aloud. Then he or she will read *one* of the definitions on the card.

4. Your teacher will ask for a show of hands to indicate whether you *accept* or *reject* the definition. Be prepared to defend your vote!

Link It: Make Word-to-World Connections

10 Things I Love About You

Directions: Pick a person and write sentences to describe things you love about him or her. Use all ten vocabulary words in your sentences—a task that requires you to get creative. For instance, *haughty* may not seem to be a desirable trait, so how could you use it to describe something you love about someone?

One final note—when you write your list, you can change the person's name to protect your privacy!

Master It: Use Words in Meaningful Ways

Set Me Free—In Verse!

Directions: Free verse is a type of poetry that does not use a set rhyme pattern or rhythm. On the next page is an example of free verse. Notice that the lines share a common theme and similar structure, but there is no rhyme or rhythm.

Crazy Little Thing

Elated by squeaky toys,

Euphoric over smelly socks,

Attentive to bugs,

Amiable as Cupid:

My dog, Zipper.

Create your own poem, written in free verse, using some of the vocabulary words. A fun way to start is to take phrases and sentences from your work in the 10 Things I Love About You activity (page 199). Edit and rearrange these phrases and sentences to form a poem. Then add the finishing touch: a title. Share your creation with classmates in a poetry festival.

Wrapping Up: Review What You've Learned

Here's a brief summary of what you've studied in this chapter.

> Many words have more than one meaning. Familiar words often have less familiar additional meanings.

> When you use a word literally, you mean exactly what you say. When you use a word figuratively, you are expressing an idea creatively, not literally.

> Writers use figurative language to create a striking mental image or make an idea memorable. When you read figurative language, you must interpret the meaning instead of just defining the words.

> Such describing words as *nice*, *great*, and *terrible* give only a general idea of meaning. They are not precise. Use specific descriptive words when you write and speak, in order to convey your ideas more clearly.

Flaunt It: Show Your Word Understanding

In the following exercises, you'll demonstrate your understanding of each vocabulary word. You will use vocabulary words, or forms of the words, to complete sentences and to write sentences of your own.

A Sentence Completion

Directions: Circle the letter of the word that best completes each sentence.

1. Many people don't get Cody's sense of humor, but I think his dry wit is _____.

   a. pathetic   **b.** haphazard
   c. delirious   **d.** hilarious

2. How can you be so _____ first thing in the morning? It takes me at least two hours to wake up.

   a. inaccessible   **b.** sinister
   c. energetic   **d.** sparse

3. Mr. Heathrow is _____ for giving a lot of homework just before a holiday weekend.

   a. steadfast   **b.** notorious
   c. drastic   **d.** elated

4. Sticking a wad of chewing gum in your enemy's hair was a/an _____ thing to do.

   a. juvenile   **b.** amiable
   c. resourceful   **d.** attentive

5. The locusts were _____, swarming across the fields and stripping the crops of leaves.

   a. sparse   **b.** ruthless
   c. inaccessible   **d.** accommodating

B Word Choice

Directions: Underline the word that best completes each sentence.

6. Your loss of your sneakers is a real (*accessory*, *tragedy*, *blemish*), seeing as how you have five other pairs at home in your closet.

7. I'm sorry to (*annihilate*, *quizzical*, *pummel*) you with so many questions, but I find your experiences in the Bahamas to be fascinating.

8. I am so sick of Freddie's lies that I decided to (*annihilate*, *redeem*, *lament*) them with the truth.

9. Of all the theories on how the race car was stolen, I think your theory is the most (*plausible*, *internal*, *pathetic*).

10. The traveling carnival is on a (*tragedy*, *depression*, *circuit*) that takes it through the Southwest before it heads north.

11. The small boardwalk boutique sold charming (*accessories*, *anesthetics*, *bearings*) such as bracelets, sunhats, scarves, and earrings.

12. Grandma (*dictated*, *reproduced*, *redeemed*) her memories aloud while I typed them into a word-processing program on my computer.

13. Sailboats (*pummeled*, *lamented*, *annihilated*) the rain as they huddled against the cold, damp docks.

14. After the clerk had been rude and surly to me, I said snidely, "Thank you for being so (*inaccessible*, *quizzical*, *accommodating*)."

15. The (*bearing*, *application*, *blemish*) of sequins on the fabric can be done using a special glue or using a needle and thread.

C Writing

Directions: Follow the directions to write sentences using vocabulary words. Write your sentences on a separate sheet of paper.

16. Use *blemish* in either a literal or a figurative sense.

17. Use *redeem* to mean "to turn in for something of value."

18. Use *anesthetic* to tell about a medical procedure.

19. Use *bearing* to mean "relevance or connection."

20. Use *haughty* in a description of a person.

21. Use *euphoric* in a description of one of your favorite activities or moments.

22. Use *singular* in a statement about an event.

23. Use *ardent* to tell something about a family member.

24. Use *probe* in a statement about an investigation.

25. Use *reproduce* to mean "to make a copy of."

Chapter Extension Activities

Activities à la Carte: Extend Your Word Knowledge

The activities on this page are presented à la carte, like items on a restaurant menu, meaning that you can choose from a variety of options. Your teacher may assign an activity or let you pick the one that tempts your appetite. If time allows, you might do more than one activity. All of the activities feature the same ingredient: **exploring the meanings of words**. Dig in!

Here I Am, World

Take a piece of writing or art that you created for this chapter (such as the poem in free verse or the trading cards) and find an *outlet* for publication. For ideas, ask teachers or librarians about trust-worthy publications or Web sites. For instance, *Teen Ink* publishes writing, art, and photos by teenagers. The Web site address is www.teenink.com.

Slang Report

Some of the slang words and expressions you use are probably figu-rative uses of words. During the next week, keep a list of slang words you use and hear. Determine whether the word also has a literal meaning and what that meaning is. Report back to your class.

Play Me a Tune

Get out the poem you wrote for Set Me Free—In Verse! (page 199) and set it to music. Grab a few musicians, a lead singer, and—voila!—you've created a band with its first original song. If you are technically inclined, use the poems to create a Web site to showcase your work.

ELL Dictate = *Dictar* or *Mandar*?

Do the multiple-meaning words in this lesson have multiple mean-ings when translated into another language? Or must you translate the English word into several different words to get the range of meanings? Translate vocabulary words (and phrases using vocab-ulary words) into another language. Analyze the results and share your insights with the class.

A Chip off the Old Block

Idioms are phrases that express a thought figuratively, not literally. That is, you can't understand the phrase by looking up the individual words in a dictionary. You have to learn what the phrase means within the culture that created it. Create an idiom poster to display in class. List a dozen or so idioms and explain their meanings. Here are a few to get you started: rain cats and dogs, a sweet tooth, a green thumb, a wolf in sheep's clothing.

But Wait! That's Not All

Some vocabulary words in this chapter have more meanings than those listed here. Often, these additional meanings are associated with different parts of speech. Identify some of these words and tell your class about additional meanings.

There, They're, or *Their*?

Homonyms are words that are spelled and pronounced the same but have different meanings, such as the multiple-meaning words in this chapter. *Homographs* are spelled alike but have different meanings, origins, and sometimes pronunciations. (Compare "This fake ID card is *invalid*" and "A nurse helped the *invalid* to bathe and dress.") And then there are *homophones*, words that are pronounced alike but have different spellings and meanings, such as *hear* and *here*. To educate your classmates, create a three-column table that explains homonyms, homographs, and homo-phones.

Song in My Heart

Song lyrics are a gold mine when it comes to figurative uses of words. Examine the lyrics of some of your favorite songs, looking for words used figuratively. How does this use of a word fire your imagination, touch your heart, or dazzle your mind's eye?

The One and Only—Or Not

Is English the only language that uses words figuratively? Find out and report back to your classmates. Give examples from English and the other language to make your explanation clear.

On Second Thought

Pull out a piece of writing that you are working on for a class or other project. Pump up the word power in the piece by using descriptive words with clear meanings and by using words figuratively. Then pat yourself on the back for using tools of the trade.

Round-Robin

Get together with a group of friends and create limited editions of your best work from this chapter (poems, artwork, ideas). One way to do this is to photocopy each person's work and bind the pages together as a booklet for each friend. For colorful artwork, you could use a color photocopier at a print shop or use colored pencils to hand-tint black-and-white copies. While you're at it, create new art or writing to add to the booklets.

Understanding Shades of Meaning

9

You might have heard the idiom "There's more than one way to skin a cat." It means that there is more than one way to accomplish a task or meet a goal. When you are studying vocabulary, this idiom (expression) can mean that there's more than one way to convey an idea.

In this chapter, you'll learn how to explore your options in expressing ideas. You'll examine connotations of words, contrast formal and informal words, and learn useful words for discussing articles, advertisements, and other media.

Objectives

In this chapter, you will learn

> How a word can seem positive or negative

> How a word can be loaded with bias or attitudes

> How a word can carry an informal or a formal tone

Sneak Peek: Preview the Lesson

Gut Reactions

In the following questions, some of the italicized words are vocabulary words in this chapter. Answer each question, giving your first response, or gut reaction. Don't worry about explaining *why* you answer the way you do. As you complete this lesson, you'll have opportunities to discuss why you might respond to a word in a particular way.

1. Which is more likely to be effective—asking your parent if a *horde* of friends can come over, or if a *group* of friends can come over? _____

2. Do you enjoy seeing a friend *smirk* at you? _____

3. Which expression shows the most sensitivity: saying that a pet *dropped dead, passed away, bit the dust,* or *kicked the bucket*? _____

4. With a friend, would you say that you didn't *comprehend* a joke, or that you didn't *get it*? _____

5. Do you think the queen of England would ever say, "*Oops, my bad*"? _____

Vocabulary Mini-Lesson: Words Have Feelings

Many words have meanings that are similar but not exactly the same. Compare these sentences:

> Ashley squealed when she saw what was in the box.
>
> Ashley screamed when she saw what was in the box.
>
> Ashley roared when she saw what was in the box.
>
> Ashley shrieked when she saw what was in the box.

All four sentences describe the same event. Read the sentences again. What effect does changing a single word have on the image in your mind?

Here's another example:

> Chris stumbled down the stairs.
>
> Chris plunged down the stairs.
>
> Chris tumbled down the stairs.
>
> Chris crashed down the stairs.

Again, changing one word changes your sense of the sentence. *Stumble* may make you think of sleepily getting out of bed and walking unsteadily down the stairs. *Tumble*, however, probably brings to mind tripping over something and falling head over heels. *Plunge* suggests descending with speed or haste. Even though the words are similar in meaning, the feelings and images associated with them are different.

To talk about the feelings associated with words, you'll find it helpful to understand two terms: denotation and connotation. The **denotation** of a word is its exact, literal meaning. For example, the denotation of *descend* is "to move from a higher place to a lower one."

In addition to denotations, many (but not all) words have connotations. The **connotation** of a word is the impression the word makes in our mind. It's a feeling that is *suggested* but not stated. For example, look again at the following sentences:

Ashley squealed when she saw what was in the box.

Squealed has a different connotation from *roared* or *shrieked*. *Squeal* is generally a less serious word than *roar* or *shriek*. Someone may squeal with delight, for example. *Roar* and *shriek*, by comparison, are usually associated with strong emotions, such as anger or fear.

Chris crashed down the stairs.

Crash suggests noise or force and has a more serious connotation than *stumble*, for example. Perhaps *crash* makes you think of a group of friends making a racket as they come running down the stairs and out the front door. In other words, a writer wouldn't use a word like *crash* to suggest someone quietly descending.

Look at these pairs of sentences. What is the denotation of the underlined words? Does each word also have a connotation? If so, do you think the connotation is generally positive or negative?

Anthony is cunning. His sister is clever.

Alexis has a plan. Her friend has a scheme.

There is a mob of people outside the store. There is a crowd of people inside.

All of the words in List 31 have connotations. Read the example sentences carefully. Use the context to help you understand whether the word has a positive or negative connotation.

Words to Know: Vocabulary Lists and Activities

What words can you think of that have a specific connotation, or feeling, along with the literal definition? In this section, you'll study ten such words.

List 31   Words with Positive and Negative Connotations

Read each word, what it means, and how it's used. Ask yourself which words imply something negative and which ones imply something positive.

Word	What It Means	How It's Used
aggressive *(adj)* uh-GREH-siv	inclined to take action; ready to attack	Eric's *aggressive* nature led to quarrels with other students.
aloof *(adj)* uh-LOOF	distant; reserved	Everyone joined in the fun except Pat, who remained *aloof* from the group.
arrogant *(adj)* A-ruh-guhnt	self-important and disdainful of others; haughty	George is so *arrogant* that he won't even take responsibility for his mistakes.
bland *(adj)* bland	uninteresting; boring; dull	The book reviewer criticized the novelist for her *bland* writing style.
consistent *(adj)* kuhn-SIS-tuhnt	the same in principles or practices; not varying; steady	Voters prefer candidates who remain *consistent* in their position on key issues.
horde *(n)* hawrd	crowd; swarm	Holiday sales attract a *horde* of shoppers.
indifferent *(adj)* in-DIH-fuhrnt	showing no concern; uncaring	Taylor feels sorry for the puppy, but Jennifer seems *indifferent*.
ingenious *(adj)* in-JEEN-yuhs	clever; creative	The digital camera is an *ingenious* invention.
smirk *(v)* smurk	to smile in an annoyingly self-satisfied way	"I warned you this would happen, didn't I?" Sean said, *smirking*.
wily *(adj)* WYE-lee	crafty; sly	The *wily* lawyer tricked the witness into revealing his secret.

Own It: Develop Your Word Understanding

Connotations

Directions: In a small group, share your ideas about the connotation of each vocabulary word. Start by having one person read a word aloud. Make sure everyone understands the word's meaning. Then tell the group whether the word has mostly positive (pleasant) connotations to you or mostly negative (unpleasant) connotations.

To help one another identify connotations, ask questions such as, "Would you want me to describe you as *aloof* ?" and "Would you rather be called *ingenious* or *wily*?" Don't be surprised if some people disagree about the connotations of some words.

Based on the group discussion, complete the ten organizers that follow. First, classify each word's connotation as positive or negative. Then explain your answer by telling *why* you think the word carries mainly pleasant or unpleasant overtones.

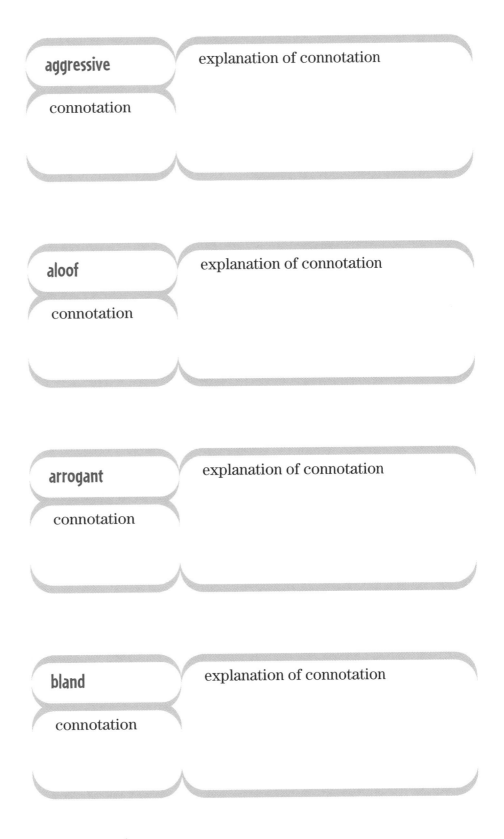

aggressive

connotation

explanation of connotation

aloof

connotation

explanation of connotation

arrogant

connotation

explanation of connotation

bland

connotation

explanation of connotation

consistent

connotation

explanation of connotation

horde

connotation

explanation of connotation

indifferent

connotation

explanation of connotation

ingenious

connotation

explanation of connotation

smirk

connotation

explanation of connotation

wily	explanation of connotation
connotation	

I'm <u>wily</u> when it comes to getting out of a jam. One <u>ingenious</u> idea I had was to put a bandage on my left thumb and tell my mom I sprained it playing basketball, so that I wouldn't have to help shovel the snow in the driveway. Her response: no texting for a week!

Link It: Make Word-to-World Connections

Welcome to My World

Directions: In this activity, you'll work alone and then with a group to link vocabulary words to your world. Here's what to do:

1. Play around with the vocabulary words, using them to make statements about yourself, friends, family members, your neighborhood, or other aspects of your life. Write at least five sentences using vocabulary words.

2. Choose three sentences that best describe your world. Cut your paper in strips, one sentence per strip.

3. In a small group, jumble everyone's sentences in a box. Take turns pulling out a sentence, reading it aloud, and guessing whose life it describes.

Master It: Use Words in Meaningful Ways

Ad Campaign

Directions: Imagine that you work for an advertising agency. You must develop an ad campaign for a client's product, and you must present your ideas in a meeting. To prepare for the meeting, follow these steps:

1. Divide a poster board down the center. On one half, you'll create an advertisement for a product of your choosing (shoes, a music CD, food, or the like). On the other half, you'll explain why the advertisement will be effective.

2. Use art supplies, magazine cutouts, and other materials to create an ad for the product.

3. List five reasons why the ad will be effective. Use some of the vocabulary words to help express these reasons.

4. Present your poster and ideas in a small group or to the whole class, as directed by your teacher. Give one another feedback. Who knows—perhaps you have a future advertising executive in your midst!

Vocabulary Mini-Lesson: Words Contain Messages

Writers choose their words carefully. They know that the connotations of words shape readers' thoughts and opinions. Compare these two sentences:

The young artist surprised people with her unusual paintings.

The young artist shocked people with her weird paintings.

Which sentence do you think was written by an admirer of the artist? How do you know?

Words like *shocked* and *weird* have negative connotations, while *surprised* and *unusual* have a positive or neutral feeling. A writer can send an unspoken message to readers by choosing the words that express his or her own point of view. Unless you think about the connotations of words, you might not even realize a message is being sent!

Such unspoken messages are everywhere. They appear in newspaper and magazine articles, in television and radio commercials, and in printed advertisements. Be on the lookout for them. Think carefully about what you read and hear. Watch for words that are meant to win you over or persuade you to act or think in a certain way.

The words in List 32 relate to the sending of messages through written and spoken communication. You can use these words when you discuss articles and advertisements. These words will also help you think about the ways people try to persuade one another.

Words to Know: Vocabulary Lists and Activities

The first list in this chapter contained words that are loaded with feelings. The following list contains words that will help you *notice* and analyze feelings and messages in advertisements and articles that you read, in school and beyond.

List 32   Words and Messages

Read each word, what it means, and how it's used.

Word	What It Means	How It's Used
biased *(adj)* BIE-uhst	reflecting personal opinion or prejudice; favoring a particular viewpoint	The speaker's choice of words makes clear that she is *biased* against school uniforms.
censorship *(n)* SEN-ser-ship	system or practice of examining and removing what is considered objectionable (You learned the suffix *-ship* in Chapter 2, List 5.)	In some countries, government *censorship* of the news prevents citizens from learning the truth about events.
credible *(adj)* KREH-duh-buhl	believable; plausible	Police disregarded the boy's version of the accident because his account was not *credible*.
euphemism *(n)* YOO-fuh-mi-zuhm	mild or inoffensive expression substituted for one that is unpleasant, harsh, or objectionable	"Pass away" is a *euphemism* for "die."

continued

generalization (n) jen-er-uh-luh-ZAY-shuhn	a broad conclusion drawn from limited facts, often one that is not well supported	"Politicians cannot be trusted" is a *generalization* that does not apply to all politicians.
infer *(v)* in-FUR	to conclude from available information	Seeing dark clouds and hearing a rumble of thunder, we *inferred* that a storm was coming.
persuasive *(adj)* per-SWAY-siv	able to persuade; convincing (You learned the suffix *-ive* in Chapter 2, List 7.)	The lawyer's arguments were *persuasive* enough to convince the jury.
propaganda *(n)* prah-puh-GAN-duh	information spread for the purpose of convincing people to accept or reject certain ideas	The dictator's *propaganda* was intended to make citizens believe that he was not at fault for the nation's economic problems.
rhetorical question *(n)* ri-TAWR-i-kuhl KWES-chuhn	a question asked only for effect, not to get an answer	When Sarah's father asked, "Do you want to be grounded for the rest of the year?" he was asking a *rhetorical question*.
stereotype *(n)* STER-ee-uh-type	an oversimplified, often unfair, notion or way of thinking, as of a person or group, held by a number of people	Such familiar television characters as the goofy father and the brainy computer nerd are *stereotypes*.

Tip

To detect unspoken messages, pay close attention to the key words that writers and speakers choose to express their ideas. Keep in mind that nouns, verbs, adjectives, and adverbs can *all* have shades of meaning. Always consider both the denotation *and* the connotation of these words.

Own It: Develop Your Word Understanding

Mix and Match

Directions: In this activity, you will mingle with classmates, trying to match vocabulary words with their definitions. Here's what to do.

1. Your teacher will write each vocabulary word on an index card. On separate cards, he or she will write the definitions. Then the cards will be jumbled together in a box.

2. You take one card from the box. You'll have either a vocabulary word or a definition.

3. Move around the classroom to find the person who has the definition of your vocabulary word, or the word that goes with your definition.

4. Together, write an explanation of the key word using your own words and examples.

5. In a class discussion, share your explanation. Also explain how easy or difficult it was to match up the word with the definition during the mixer. Which words or definitions were easy to eliminate? Which made you think hard about whether they were a correct match?

Link It: Make Word-to-World Connections

Fame or Shame?

Directions: In this activity, you'll link vocabulary words to the real world and then sort your findings between the Hall of Fame and the Hall of Shame. Here's how the activity works.

1. Examine the world around you, looking for links between vocabulary words and the world. For instance, you may identify a speech that is *biased* against a certain age group. You may see an instance of *censorship*, you may hear a *euphemism* or *rhetorical question*, or you may notice a *stereotype* that offends (or delights) you.

2. Bring one example from step 1, or clear notes about the example, to class.

3. Share your example of the word-world link. Then let the class vote. Does your example belong on the Wall of Fame or the Wall of Shame? For instance, an offensive stereotype belongs on the Wall of Shame. A persuasive ad for drinking milk may belong on the Wall of Fame.

Master It: Use Words in Meaningful Ways

Critic's Choice

Directions: In this activity, you'll become an entertainment critic and write a review for your classmates. Here's what to do.

1. Choose a movie, book, or music album to review.
2. Watch the movie, read the book, or listen to the album. As you do so, takes notes on strong points, weak points, remarkable sections or ideas, and so on. Keep the vocabulary words handy and let them inspire some of your comments.
3. Write your review. A useful format to follow is to (1) introduce the item being reviewed, (2) describe several strong/positive qualities, (3) mention a need for improvement (if any), and (4) give your overall impression. (For instance, "This book will appeal to animal lovers.") Aim for a reading time of *3–4 minutes*.
4. With your teacher, plan a Critic's Choice event in class, when you snack on popcorn while people share their reviews. Afterward, you'll have enough entertainment recommendations to keep you busy for a month!

Vocabulary Mini-Lesson: Words Carry Tone

When was the last time you wore your fanciest clothes? Perhaps you attended a wedding or a special religious ceremony. No doubt, you selected your clothes with care. You didn't just pull on a sweatshirt and an old pair of jeans. You dressed in a way that was appropriate for the occasion.

Language is not so different from clothing. Writers and speakers choose words that are appropriate for the occasion. For instance, in an essay for English about a novel that you enjoyed reading, you might describe the book as "thrilling" or "gripping." If you were talking to another student, though, you might simply say the book was "awesome."

Just as you wouldn't wear jeans to a wedding, you wouldn't use slang for a school essay. Similarly, writers don't use chatty, casual language when they create serious documents, such as reports or business letters. Instead, they choose more formal language. Such language may not always be the simplest way to express ideas. However, it does add "weight" to what is being said. Formal words send an unspoken message: *This is a serious matter.*

Words to Know: Vocabulary Lists and Activities

List 33   Formal Words

As you read these words, think about the kinds of situations in which you might use them. Read each word, what it means, and how it's used.

Word	What It Means	How It's Used
adequate *(adj)* A-di-kwit	enough; sufficient	Young children are not allowed in the swimming pool without *adequate* adult supervision.
competent *(adj)* KOM-pi-tuhnt	having the necessary ability or qualities; qualified; capable	A *competent* mechanic will be able to repair the car.
comprehend *(v)* kom-pri-HEND	understand; grasp	The amount of damage caused by the hurricane is difficult to *comprehend*.
conventional *(adj)* kuhn-VEN-shuh-nl	usual or standard; traditional	When *conventional* treatments failed, doctors gave the patient an experimental drug.
criteria *(n, plural)* kry-TEER-ee-uh	the standards used for judging or evaluation something (singular: *criterion*)	The rubric listed the five *criteria* used for assessing our persuasive essays.
impact *(n)* IM-pakt	influence; effect	The *impact* of computer technology on our society is beyond measure.
inquiry *(n)* IN-kwuh-ree	investigation; search for information	Government officials launched an *inquiry* into the charges of wrongdoing.
jargon *(n)* JAR-guhn	the technical or specialized language of a particular activity or group of people	Only doctors and nurses can understand medical *jargon*.
profound *(adj)* pruh-FOUND	very great; significant; far-reaching	The invention of the printing press had a *profound* effect on civilization.
regrettable *(adj)* ri-GREH-tuh-buhl	deserving regret; unfortunate	It was *regrettable* that the weather was so stormy on graduation day.

Own It: Develop Your Word Understanding

Black Tie or Blue Jeans?

Directions: In this activity, you'll explore formal and informal synonyms of the vocabulary words. Grab a partner and a thesaurus, and complete these steps for each organizer:

1. *In the left side:* Write a sentence or describe a situation to show how you could use the vocabulary word. Underneath that, write one (or more) **formal** synonyms of the vocabulary word. For instance, a formal synonym of *adequate* is *sufficient.*

2. *In the right side:* Write a few **informal** synonyms of the vocabulary word. Slang expressions are fine here. For instance, informal synonyms of *adequate* are *good enough* and *okay*. Finally, write a sentence or describe a situation in which you could use one of the informal synonyms.

adequate

how I might use this formal word:

some less formal synonyms:

how I might use one of these synonyms:

a formal synonym of this word:

competent

how I might use this formal word:

some less formal synonyms:

how I might use one of these synonyms:

a formal synonym of this word:

comprehend

how I might use this formal word:

some less formal synonyms:

how I might use one of these synonyms:

a formal synonym of this word:

conventional

how I might use this formal word:

some less formal synonyms:

how I might use one of these synonyms:

a formal synonym of this word:

criteria

how I might use this formal word:

some less formal synonyms:

how I might use one of these synonyms:

a formal synonym of this word:

impact

how I might use this formal word:

some less formal synonyms:

how I might use one of these synonyms:

a formal synonym of this word:

inquiry

how I might use this formal word:

some less formal synonyms:

how I might use one of these synonyms:

a formal synonym of this word:

jargon

how I might use this formal word:

some less formal synonyms:

how I might use one of these synonyms:

a formal synonym of this word:

profound

how I might use this formal word:

some less formal synonyms:

how I might use one of these synonyms:

a formal synonym of this word:

> **regrettable**

how I might use this formal word:	some less formal synonyms:
	how I might use one of these synonyms:
a formal synonym of this word:	

Link It: Make Word-to-World Connections

Cartoon Convention

Directions: Why is it funny to see dogs dressed in suits and playing pool? Probably because the two things are so mismatched that the combination is humorous.

Words and situations work similarly. You might find yourself laughing when a friend uses unnecessarily formal language. Likewise, you might laugh when someone uses slang during a serious situation. (Think of someone calling the president of the United States "dude.")

Tune up your funny bone and create your own single-frame cartoon. Use a vocabulary word in the caption. To get your ideas flowing, think about situations in which the vocabulary words would be humorously out of place. It may help to brainstorm ideas with a friend.

You can sketch your own cartoon panel, use a photograph or magazine cutout, or ask an artistic friend to help you carry out your vision.

Display your creation during a Cartoon Convention in class.

Master It: Use Words in Meaningful Ways

In All Seriousness

Directions: Rules govern our lives at school, home, work, and play, no matter our age. Some rules are fair and necessary; others may be unfair or unnecessary. Think of a rule that you must follow that seems unfair or unnecessary to you. Write a formal letter to the person who enforces this rule, explaining why you think the rule is not needed. In your letter, use several vocabulary words (or forms of them).

Give a copy of your letter to your teacher. It's up to you whether to deliver a copy of the letter to its addressee.

Wrapping Up: Review What You've Learned

Here's a brief summary of what you've studied in this chapter.

> Many words have meanings that are similar but not exactly the same. Often when two words have similar meanings, one of the words seems to have a negative feeling while the other leaves a more positive impression.

> The **denotation** of a word is its exact, literal meaning. Many words also have connotations. The **connotation** is the impression the word makes in our mind. It is a feeling that is suggested but not stated.

> By choosing a word with a positive or negative connotation, the writer can change the reader's understanding of the sentence.

> Writers choose their words carefully because they know that the connotations of words shape readers' thoughts and opinions.

A writer can send an unspoken message—positive or negative— by choosing words that express his or her own feelings.

> Unspoken messages appear in both written and spoken communication, such as newspaper and magazine articles, television commercials, and printed advertisements. Such messages are meant to persuade people to act or think in a certain way.

> Writers and speakers choose words that are appropriate for the occasion. In serious circumstances, they don't use chatty, casual language. Instead, they use more formal language that adds "weight" to what is being said.

Chapter Review Exercises

Flaunt It: Show Your Word Understanding

In the following exercises, you'll demonstrate your understanding of each vocabulary word. You will use vocabulary words, or forms of the words, to complete sentences and to write sentences of your own.

A Sentence Completion

Directions: Circle the letter of the word that best completes each sentence.

1. Jared, who pushes and pinches the other children, learned his _____ behavior from his older brothers.

   a. aggressive   **b.** credible
   c. indifferent   **d.** aloof

2. When Mrs. Lynwood said that I was being "let go" from the volunteer position, I understood the _____ to mean "fired."

   a. propaganda   **b.** inquiry
   c. euphemism   **d.** rhetorical question

3. For the dance, Lucy chose a _____ dress for an elegant and classic look.

   a. bland   **b.** conventional
   c. regrettable   **d.** stereotype

4. The _____ boys found a way to sneak into the warehouse and make off with a case of double-fudge cookies.

   a. adequate   **b.** profound
   c. biased   **d.** wily

5. The cheerleading performance was judged based on three different _____ .

   a. criteria   **b.** impact
   c. censorship   **d.** infer

B Matching

Directions: Match the underlined word to its definition. Write the letter of the definition on the line provided.

_____ 6. Based on the Warren family's frequent "family game nights," I made the generalization that they like spending time together.

_____ 7. Antonio's argument was so persuasive that his parents agreed immediately to buy him the art supplies.

_____ 8. There's no need to smirk just because you won the game.

_____ 9. Bailey is a fantastic baseball pitcher, but she is annoyingly arrogant about her skill.

_____ 10. After I left a slice of pizza on the counter overnight, a horde of ants invaded the kitchen.

_____ 11. Molly's idea for making tote bags out of recycled dresses and blue jeans was ingenious.

_____ 12. When it comes to designing Web pages, Russ is not just competent; he is outstanding!

_____ 13. If you do not comprehend the instructions, raise your hand so that a teacher can help you.

_____ 14. When Garrett took up skate-boarding, he started using a lot of jargon such as "mongo," "goofy," and "half-pipe."

_____ 15. First you said that you found the wallet, and then you said that you borrowed it; your story is not consistent.

a. a broad conclusion drawn from limited facts

b. the technical or specialized language of a particular activity or group of people

c. having the necessary ability or qualities; qualified

d. self-important and disdainful of others; haughty

e. clever; creative

f. understand; grasp

g. able to persuade; convincing

h. crowd; swarm

I. the same in principles or practices; not varying; steady

J. to smile in an annoyingly self-satisfied way

Writing

Directions: Choose *one* of the following nouns as a topic for writing. Then write a paragraph that gives information or expresses an opinion about the topic. In your paragraph, use the noun you chose and at least *three* adjectives listed below. You may use additional nouns and adjectives from the lists as needed. Write your paragraph on a separate sheet of paper.

Nouns		Adjectives	
horde	stereotype	aggressive	biased
censorship	criteria	aloof	credible
euphemism	impact	arrogant	persuasive
generalization	inquiry	bland	adequate
propaganda	jargon	consistent	competent
rhetorical question	smirk	indifferent	conventional
		ingenious	profound
		wily	regrettable

Activities à la Carte: Extend Your Word Knowledge

The activities on this page are presented à la carte, like items on a restaurant menu, meaning that you can choose from a variety of options. Your teacher may assign an activity or let you pick the one that tempts your appetite. If time allows, you might do more than one activity. All of the activities feature the same ingredient: **shades of meaning in words**. Dig in!

Jargon Collector

Choose a profession or field of work that interests you and compile a list of jargon used in that field. Medical jargon, computer jargon, sports jargon, and political jargon are just a few possible areas to explore.

I Have a Dream

With vocabulary words in mind, examine a famous or inspirational speech. Does the speaker use formal or informal language? Is the speaker *biased* in some way? Does he or she use *rhetorical questions* as a *persuasive* technique? Point out parts of the speech that help you answer these and other questions. Report back to your class, or get permission to give an oral report in a related class, such as history.

Wordplay

Some people invent secret codes, and others learn the slang of new friends. Some people buy boxes of magnetic words and arrange them into poems on the refrigerator. Why? People like to play with the shades of meaning in words. Choose an art form and play with some words of your choosing. You might make a collage of words ripped from newspaper headlines, for example, or print words from this chapter and adorn them with images that they inspire. Display your wordplay in your classroom.

What Did You Just Say?

A professional translator must master not only the vocabulary of a second language but also connotations of words in that language.

Find out about the career path of translation and report back to your class. What kinds of jobs can a translator get? Why is connotation so important to the job of translation?

 ## What He Said Was . . .

Present a translation demonstration to your classmates. Have a partner explain something to the class in a language other than English. After every sentence or so, your partner pauses to let you translate what he or she is saying. Afterward, ask your classmates for feedback about connotations of particular English words you used. Also ask your partner if your translation captured connotations of his or her words accurately.

Devil's Advocate

Find an advertisement or argument that seems convincing. Then play devil's advocate by making a case for the opposite point of view. Use vocabulary words from the lists in this chapter to inspire your analysis. To take it a step further, stage a debate in class by having a friend argue in support of the advertisement while you argue against it.

Word Doctor

Pull out a paper or project that you are writing for a class. Edit your word choices by replacing informal and slang words with formal words and expressions. To create a specific mood in your readers, fine-tune your word choices based on their connotations.

Encore! Encore!

In this book, you've studied scores of vocabulary words. Which words confounded you? Delighted you? Inspired you? Choose 52 words and use them to create a Word-of-the-Week calendar. You can recycle an old calendar by pasting new paper on it, use scrap paper and a hole punch, or design and print out pages. For each word, give a pronunciation guide, a definition, and an example sentence.

Appendix

Using a Dictionary

A dictionary entry usually gives you the following information about a word:

> The pronunciation and how it's divided into syllables. The pronunciation is either given as a respelling, which shows you how to sound out the word (as done in this book), or it is given using what's called diacritical marks, or symbols. (Dictionaries with diacritical marks have keys that show you what those marks mean.) Hyphens or spaces are used to show how a word is divided into syllables.

> The part of speech

> The different definitions, sometimes with sample phrases or definitions

> Other forms of the word parts of speech

> Synonyms

---

de•cay (di-KAY)

Etymology: Middle English, from Latin *decadere*, to fall, sink

Date: 15th century

decay *(v)* **1** to decline **2** to decrease slowly in size, amount, or force **3** to fall into ruin **4** to decompose

Synonym: rot, spoil

—**decayer** *(n)*

decay *(n)* **1** a slow decline in strength or excellence **2** a wasting or wearing away **3** a decline in health **4** rot **5** ruin

---

Glossary

A

ablaze (uh-BLAYZ) *(adv)*: on fire; burning

abstract (ab-STRAKT) *(adj)*: not representing an actual object or person

accessible (ik-SEH-suh-buhl) *(adj)*: capable of being reached or entered

accessory (ik-SEH-suh-ree) *(n)*: something of secondary importance that adds to an object's usefulness, appearance, or comfort; a person who assists in or contributes to a crime

accommodating (uh-KAH-muh-day-ting) *(adj)*: willing to please; obliging; helpful

accomplice (uh-KOM-plis) *(n)*: someone who knowingly participates in the commission of a crime

acquit (uh-KWIT) *(v)*: to declare to be innocent of a crime

adaptation (a-dap-TAY-shuhn) *(n)*: a composition rewritten or otherwise changed to make it suitable for a new use

addictive (uh-DIK-tiv) *(adj)*: causing addiction

adequate (A-di-kwit) *(adj)*: enough; sufficient

adhere (ad-HEER) *(v)*: to stay attached; stick

adherence (ad-HERE-uhns) *(n)*: obedience; observance

adjacent (uh-JAY-suhnt) *(adj)*: next to; nearby

admirable (AD-mer-uh-buhl) *(adj)*: deserving to be admired or praised

admittance (ad-MIH-tunts) *(n)*: permission to enter

adrift (uh-DRIFT) *(adv)*: floating freely; drifting

adversely (ad-VURS-lee) *(adv)*: in a harmful way; unfavorably; negatively

advocate (AD-vuh-kate) *(v)*: to plead in support of

aggression (uh-GREH-shuhn) *(n)*: hostile, threatening, or destructive behavior

aggressive (uh-GREH-siv) *(adj)*: inclined to take action; ready to attack

agritourism (ah-gri-TOOR-i-zuhm) *(n)*: the touring or visiting of farms or agricultural areas, usually with some participation in farm activities

allege (uh-LEJ) *(v)*: to state or claim something before proving or without proving

aloof (uh-LOOF) *(adj)*: distant; reserved

amiable (AY-mee-uh-buhl) *(adj)*: friendly; good-natured

amnesia (am-NEE-zhuh) *(n)*: loss of memory, usually as a result of an accident or illness

amorous (AH-meh-ruhs) *(adj)*: relating to or showing love

anesthetic (a-nuhs-THEH-tik) *(n)*: a substance, such as a drug, that causes an insensitivity to pain

annihilate (uh-NIE-uh-late) *(v)*: to destroy completely

anonymous (uh-NAH-nuh-muhs) *(adj)*: not named; unidentified

anthropology (an-thruh-PAH-luh-jee) *(n)*: the scientific study of human beings and their culture

antibiotic (an-tee-by-AH-tik) *(n)*: a substance that destroys germs, used to treat diseases

antidote (AN-ti-doht) *(n)*: a remedy to counteract the effects of a poison

antiseptic (an-tuh-SEP-tik) *(n)*: a substance that fights germs so as to prevent infection

antonym (AN-tuh-nim) *(n)*: a word that means the opposite of another word

application (a-pli-KAY-shuhn) *(n)*: act or manner of applying or using; relevance; connection; a request, or the form used to make a request

archaeologist (ahr-kee-AH-luh-jist) *(n)*: a scientist who studies human life and activities of the past

ardent (AHR-dnt) *(adj)*: passionate; enthusiastic

arrogant (A-ruh-guhnt) *(adj)*: self-important and disdainful of others; haughty

artifact (AHR-tuh-fakt) *(n)*: a human-made object

attentive (uh-TEN-tiv) *(adj)*: paying attention to the needs of others; considerate

attentively (uh-TEN-tiv-lee) *(adv)*: paying close attention; carefully; alertly

avert (uh-VURT) *(v)*: to keep from happening; prevent; avoid

B

baby boomer (BAY-bee BOO-mer) *(n)*: someone born during a period of increased birth rates (a "baby boom"), especially a person born during the period after World War II, 1946–1964

basin (BAY-suhn) *(n)*: the land drained by a river and its branches

bearing (BAIR-ing) *(n)*: manner of carrying oneself; behavior; relation; connection; relevance

belligerence (buh-LIJ-er-runts) *(n)*: aggressively hostile attitude; hostility

benign (bi-NINE) *(adj)*: not threatening to health (particularly: not becoming cancerous)

biased (BIE-uhst) *(adj)*: reflecting personal opinion or prejudice; favoring a particular viewpoint

biodiesel (BIE-oh-DEE-zuhl) *(n)*: fuel that is like diesel fuel but is made out of vegetable substances like soybean oil

bioweapon (BIE-oh WEH-puhn) *(n)*: a harmful biological agent, such as a disease-spreading microorganism, used as a weapon

bizarre (bi-ZAHR) *(adj)*: strikingly odd or unusual; strange

bland (bland) *(adj)*: uninteresting; boring; dull

blemish (BLEH-mish) *(n)*: a mark, spot, or flaw that detracts from the appearance

blog (blahg) *(n)*: a journal or diary posted online by the writer

Bluetooth (BLEW-tooth) *(n)*: wireless technology for interconnecting electronic devices

bodega (boh-DAY-guh) *(n)*: a small grocery store

boutique (boo-TEEK) *(n)*: a small shop that sells fashionable, generally expensive, items

boycott (BOY-kot) *(v)*: to join with others to refuse to deal with, purchase, or use

C

captivate (KAP-tuh-vate) *(v)*: to influence through an irresistible appeal or attraction; capture the attention of

carcinogen (kahr-SI-nuh-juhn) *(n)*: a substance that causes cancer

cashmere (KAZH-meer) *(n)*: fine wool obtained from goats of the Kashmir region of southern Asia

censorship (SEN-ser-ship) *(n)*: system or practice of examining and removing what is considered objectionable

chimera (ki-MEER-uh) *(n)*: a made-up dream or illusion in the mind

chronic (KRAH-nik) *(adj)*: lasting a long time or recurring often

chronicle (KRAH-ni-kuhl) *(n)*: a historical account of events arranged in the order in which they occurred

chronological (krah-nih-LAH-jih kuhl) *(adj)*: arranged in order of occurrence

circuit (SUR-kit) *(n)*: the act of moving around; circular passage; the complete path by which an electric current flows

circumference (ser-KUHM-fer-ents) *(n)*: the line bounding a circle

circumnavigate (sur-kuhm-NAH-vi-gate) *(v)*: to go completely around

cliché (klee-SHAY) *(n)*: an expression or idea that has been worn out by too much use

cologne (kuh-LONE) *(n)*: a perfumed liquid

coma (KOH-muh) *(n)*: a state of prolonged unconsciousness caused by injury or disease

communism (KOM-yuh-nih-zuhm) *(n)*: economic system under which property is owned by the community as a whole

competent (KOM-pi-tuhnt) *(adj)*: having the necessary ability or qualities; qualified; capable

comprehend (kom-pri-HEND) *(v)*: understand; grasp

connoisseur (kah-nuh-SUR) *(n)*: someone who is an expert in a particular area, such as art or food

consistent (kuhn-SIS-tuhnt) *(adj)*: the same in principles or practices; not varying; steady

contraband (KON-truh-band) *(n)*: illegally imported or exported goods

contradict (kon-truh-DIKT) *(v)*: to state the opposite of; disagree with

contrite (kuhn-TRITE) *(adj)*: feeling or showing sorrow or regret; regretful

controversy (KON-truh-vur-see) *(n)*: dispute; disagreement

conventional (kuhn-VEN-shuh-nl) *(adj)*: usual or standard; traditional

counterclockwise (koun-ter-KLOK-wize) *(adv)*: in the direction opposite to that in which the hands of a clock move

coup d'état (koo-day-TAH) *(n)*: the sudden, violent overthrow of a ruler or government by a small group of people

credible (KREH-duh-buhl) *(adj)*: believable; plausible

criteria (kry-TEER-ee-uh) *(n)*: the standards used for judging or evaluation something

D

decay (di-KAY) *(v)*: (of a radioactive substance) to disintegrate or become less

defendant (di-FEN-duhnt) *(n)*: a person sued by another or accused of a crime

dejected (di-JEK-tid) *(adj)* unhappy; discouraged

delirious (di-LEER-ee-uhs) *(adj)*: in a state of excited confusion

denim (DEH-nuhm) *(n)*: a sturdy, durable fabric, used to make jeans and other clothing

depression (di-PREH-shuhn) *(n)*: an emotional condition characterized by such feelings as sadness and hopelessness; a low or sunken place in a surface

detract (di-TRAKT) *(v)*: to reduce the quality or value of something

devastating (DE-vuh-stay-ting) *(adj)*: destructive; damaging

dictate (DIK-tate) *(v)*: to say or impose with authority; to speak or read (something) aloud for a person or machine to record

diligent (DI-lih-juhnt) *(adj)*: careful and steady; painstaking

dinghy (DING-gee) *(n)*: a small boat

diplomatic (dih-pluh-MAH-tik) *(adj)*: relating to relations between nations

diversity (di-VUR-si-tee) *(n)*: variety; mixture

divert (di-VURT) *(v)*: to turn aside; redirect

dot-com (dot-KOM) *(n)*: a company that markets its products or services mainly through the Internet

downsize (DOUN-sahyz) *(v)*: to reduce in size; usually means to reduce the number of employees in a business

drastic (DRAS-tik) *(adj)*: strong or violent in effect; severe; extreme

E

economical (eh-kuh-NAH-mi-kuhl) *(adj)*: making wise use of resources; not wasteful

edict (EE-dikt) *(n)*: an official public announcement having the force of law; decree

eject (i-JEKT) *(v)*: to remove; throw out

elated (i-LATE-id) *(adj)*: in high spirits; delighted; overjoyed

elude (i-LOOD) *(v)*: to avoid or escape

embolden (em-BOHL-duhn) *(v)*: to make bold; fill with courage

emergence (i-MUR-juhnts) *(n)*: process or fact of becoming known

emissary (EH-muh-ser-ee) *(n)*: a person sent on a mission; representative

encore (ON-kawr) *(n)*: a demand by the audience for another appearance of a performer; the appearance in response to such a demand

energetic (eh-ner-JE-tik) *(adj)*: full of or showing energy; lively

envoy (EN-voy) *(n)*: a person sent to represent one government in dealing with another; representative

epicure (EH-pi-kyoor) *(n)*: someone who is devoted to good food and drink

epidemic (eh-pih-DEH-mik) *(n)*: a rapidly spreading disease that affects a large number of people

epilogue (EH-puh-lawg) *(n)*: a concluding section added to a novel or other literary work, providing additional information

epiphyte (EH-puh-fite) *(n)*: a plant that grows on another plant

epitaph (EH-pih-taf) *(n)*: an inscription on a gravestone in memory of the person buried there

eradicate (i-RA-di-cate) *(v)*: to eliminate; wipe out

erosive (i-ROH-siv) *(adj)*: causing erosion; wearing away

euphemism (YOO-fuh-mi-zuhm) *(n)*: mild or inoffensive expression substituted for one that is unpleasant, harsh, or objectionable

euphoric (yoo-FAWR-ik) *(adj)*: having strong or exaggerated feelings of happiness or well-being

evacuate (i-VAH-kyuh-wait) *(v)*: to remove from

evasion (i-VAY-zhuhn) *(n)*: act of avoiding something; avoidance

exasperate (ig-ZAS-puh-rate) *(v)*: to annoy or make angry; irritate

exclusive (iks-KLOO-siv) *(adj)*: limited to certain people only

exhaustive (ig-ZAW-stiv) *(adj)*: thorough; comprehensive

expectation (ek-spek-TAY-shuhn) *(n)*: act or state of expecting; anticipation

expiration (ek-spuh-RAY-shuhn) *(n)*: coming to an end; termination

exposition (ek-spuh-ZIH-shun) *(n)*: writing or speech that is meant to give information or explain something

extract (ik-STRAKT) *(v)*: to draw out; pull out

F

fantasize (FAN-tuh-size) *(v)*: to imagine; daydream

fax (faks) *(v, n)*: to transmit (a copy of a document) electronically over a telephone line

festive (FES-tiv) *(adj)*: suitable for a festival or celebration

fiasco (fee-AS-koh) *(n)*: a complete failure

fluent (FLOO-uhnt) *(adj)*: able to use a language easily and expressively

foreboding (fawr-BOH-ding) *(n)*: a sign or feeling of something evil or harmful to come

foremost (FAWR-mohst) *(adj)*: leading; most important

foresight (FAWR-site) *(n)*: careful or wise thought regarding the future

forte (FOR-tay) *(n)*: something a person does especially well; strong point

fortify (FAWR-tuh-fie) *(v)*: to make strong; strengthen

frustration (fruhs-TRAY-shuhn) *(n)*: feeling of irritation or annoyance; aggravation

G

galvanize (GAL-vuh-nize) *(v)*: to stimulate, as if by electric shock; excite; rouse

generalization (jen-er-uh-luh-ZAY-shuhn) *(n)*: a broad conclusion drawn from limited facts, often one that is not well supported

genre (ZHAHN-ruh) *(n)*: a kind or type of literature, art, or music

grimace (GRI-muhs) *(v, n)*: to twist the face in an expression of displeasure or pain; frown

guerrilla (guh-RIH-luh) *(n)*: member of a force of soldiers not part of a regular military unit, who harass the enemy and cause destruction

guidance (GUY-dunts) *(n)*: process of guiding; direction

H

habitually (huh-BIH-chuh-lee) *(adv)*: regularly, as though a habit; usually

haphazard (hap-HAZ-erd) *(adj)*: without a plan; random

haughty (HAW-tee) *(adj)*: having too much pride in oneself and disdain for others

hearten (HAHR-tn) *(v)*: to raise the spirits of; encourage

heroism (HER-uh-wih-zuhm) *(n)*: the behavior or qualities of a hero

hilarious (hi-LAIR-ee-uhs) *(adj)*: very funny; uproarious

hindrance (HIN-druhnts) *(n)*: something that hinders or gets in the way; obstacle

hologram (HAH-luh-gram) *(n)*: a three-dimensional photographic image produced by means of a laser

horde (hawrd) *(n)*: crowd; swarm

I

identity (eye-DEN-ti-tee) *(n)*: individuality; uniqueness

identity theft (eye-DEN-ti-tee theft) *(n)*: the illegal use of another person's personal information for the purpose of financial gain

IED (I-E-D) *(n)*: a crudely made bomb

immortal (i-MAWR-tl) *(adj)*: living forever; everlasting

immunity (i-MYOO-ni-tee) *(n)*: the body's ability to resist germs

immunize (IH-myuh-nize) *(v)*: to make immune, as by vaccination

impact (IM-pakt) *(n)*: influence; effect

impulsively (im-PUHL-siv-lee) *(adv)*: quickly and with little or no forethought

inaccessible (in-ik-SEH-suh-buhl) *(adj)*: not capable of being reached or entered

inborn (IN-BAWRN) *(adj)*: in a person at birth; natural; instinctive

incapable (in-KAY-puh-buhl) *(adj)*: (used with *of*) not having the ability

incision (in-SIH-zuhn) *(n)*: a cut or gash; especially a cut made for surgical purposes

incompetent (in-KOM-pi-tuhnt) *(adj)*: not having enough ability or knowledge

inconclusive (in-kuhn-KLOO-siv) *(adj)*: leading to no conclusion or definite result

indifferent (in-DIH-fuhrnt) *(adj)*: showing no concern; uncaring

indispensable (in-di-SPEN-suh-buhl) *(adj)*: absolutely necessary; essential

inevitable (ih-NEV-i-tuh-buhl) *(adj)*: not to be avoided; sure to happen; unavoidable

infer (in-FUR) *(v)*: to conclude from available information

inflammation (in-fluh-MAY-shuhn) *(n)*: redness, swelling, or pain of body tissue, usually as a result of injury or irritation

inflexible (in-FLEK-suh-buhl) *(adj)*: not open to change or compromise; rigid; unyielding

infuriate (in-FYOOR-ee-ate) *(v)*: to make angry; enrage

ingenious (in-JEEN-yuhs) *(adj)*: clever; creative

inquiry (IN-kwuh-ree) *(n)*: investigation; search for information

insolent (IN-suh-luhnt) *(adj)*: boldly insulting, disrespectful, or rude

inspiration (in-spuh-RAY-shuhn) *(n)*: something that inspires; a stimulating or motivating influence

intangible (in-TAN-juh-buhl) *(adj)*: not capable of being touched; not easily defined or grasped

internal (in-TUR-nuhl) *(adj)*: relating to the inside; relating to or occurring within an organization or nation

interrelate (in-ter-ri-LATE) *(v)*: to be linked or mutually related

intricate (IN-tri-kit) *(adj)*: complicated; complex

invincible (in-VIN-suh-buhl) *(adj)*: not capable of being conquered; unbeatable

iridescent (ir-i-DEH-suhnt) *(adj)*: having a rainbowlike display of colors

irrelevant (i-REH-luh-vuhnt) *(adj)*: not related to the subject; beside the point

irreversible (ir-i-VUHR-suh-buhl) *(adj)*: not able to be reversed or changed back

J

jargon (JAR-guhn) *(n)*: the technical or specialized language of a particular activity or group of people

jovial (JOH-vee-uhl) *(adj)*: filled with good humor; cheerful

juvenile (JOO-vuh-nile) *(adj)*: childish; immature

L

lament (luh-MENT) *(v)*: to feel sorrow or regret; mourn

leach (leech) *(v)*: to dissolve and wash away

lethargy (LEH-ther-jee) *(n)*: the quality of being lazy, sluggish, and indifferent

libel (LIE-buhl) *(n)*: a published or broadcast statement that is untrue and hurts a person's reputation

likewise (LAHYK-wize) *(adv)*: in the same manner; similarly

lofty (LAWF-tee) *(adj)*: very high

luxuriant (lug-ZHOOR-ee-uhnt) *(adj)*: abundant; lush

M

malicious (muh-LIH-shuhs) *(adj)*: intentionally hurtful; mean

malware (MAL-ware) *(n)*: software designed to damage or disturb a computer's normal functioning

mesmerize (MEZ-muh-rize) *(v)*: to hypnotize; captivate; fascinate

modification (mah-duh-fuh-KAY-shuhn) *(n)*: a change; alteration or adjustment

monologue (MAH-nuh-lawg) *(n)*: a long speech made by one speaker

monorail (MAH-nuh-rale) *(n)*: a railway in which cars operate on a single rail

monotonously (muh-NAH-teh-nuhs-lee) *(adv)*: with little or no variation; in a boring or tedious way

mystify (MIS-tuh-fie) *(v)*: to puzzle; bewilder; perplex

N

nanotechnology (nah-no-tek-NAH-luh-jee) *(n)*: the design and production of microscopic electronic devices built from atoms and molecules

narcissistic (nahr-suh-SIS-tik) *(adj)*: overly concerned with oneself; self-centered; vain

nemesis (NEH-muh-sis) *(n)*: one who inflicts revenge; also, a formidable opponent

netizen (NET-uh-zuhn) *(n)*: a person who spends a substantial amount of time on the Internet

netroots (NET-roots) *(n)*: political activism conducted over the Internet, especially via blogs

nonchalant (non-shuh-LAHNT) *(adj)*: seeming to be indifferent; unconcerned

noticeable (NOH-ti-suh-buhl) *(adj)*: easily noticed; clear; obvious

notorious (noh-TAWR-ee-uhs) *(adj)*: widely known and talked about, especially unfavorably

O

onward (ON-werd) *(adv)*: toward a point ahead; forward

oral tradition (AWR-uhl tru-DIH-shuhn) *(n)*: the preservation and sharing of past knowledge through spoken communication

orangutan (uh-RANG-uh-tan) *(n)*: a large ape found in Borneo and Sumatra

outlast (out-LAST) *(v)*: to keep going or last longer than

outmaneuver (out-muh-NOO-ver) *(v)*: to plan or perform with greater skill

outspoken (out-SPOH-kuhn) *(adj)*: speaking out boldly and freely, without reserve

outward (OUT-werd) *(adv, adj)*: on or toward the outside

ownership (OH-ner-ship) *(n)*: the state or fact of being an owner

P

pander (PAN-der) *(v)*: to accommodate or satisfy the desires or weaknesses of others

paparazzi (pah-puh-RAHT-see) *(n)*: photographers who aggressively follow celebrities in order to take candid pictures

pathetic (puh-THEH-tik) *(adj)*: so unsuccessful or inadequate as to be pitiful

perjury (PUR-juh-ree) *(n)*: making a false statement in a court of law while swearing it to be true

persistent (per-SIS-tuhnt) *(adj)*: continuing; ongoing

persuasive (per-SWAY-siv) *(adj)*: able to persuade; convincing

philanthropist (fi-LAN-thruh-pist) *(n)*: someone who tries to promote human welfare, as by making charitable gifts

philosophy (fi-LAH-suh-fee) *(n)*: the study of the basic principles and beliefs underlying human knowledge and behavior

phishing (FISH-ing) *(n)*: an attempt to trick a computer user into revealing confidential personal information, which is then stolen and used illegally

plaintiff (PLAIN-tif) *(n)*: a person who brings a lawsuit against another person

plausible (PLAW-zuh-buhl) *(adj)*: reasonable; believable

podcast (pod-kast) *(n)*: a digital file distributed over the Internet to be downloaded onto computers and media players

polygon (PAH-lee-gahn) *(n)*: a closed plane figure having three or more sides and angles

polysyllabic (pah-lee-si-LAH-bik) *(adj)*: having several syllables

postpone (pohst-POHN) *(v)*: to put off until a later time; delay

postscript (POHST-skript) *(n)*: a note added to a letter following the signature

postwar (POHST-WAWR) *(adj)*: after a war

prehistoric (pree-his-TAWR-ik) *(adj)*: before recorded history

probe (prohb) *(n)*: a slender medical instrument used to explore a wound or space; an investigation; a spacecraft designed to explore and gather information about the atmosphere, outer space, or a planet

profound (pruh-FOUND) *(adj)*: very great; significant; far-reaching

propaganda (prah-puh-GAN-duh) *(n)*: information spread for the purpose of convincing people to accept or reject certain ideas

propensity (pruh-PEN-suh-tee) *(n)*: tendency; inclination

prosecute (PRAH-si-kyoot) *(v)*: to bring legal action against for the committing of a crime or breaking of a law

pseudonym (SOO-duh-nim) *(n)*: a false name

psychology (sie-KAH-luh-jee) *(n)*: the scientific study of the mind and behavior

psychosis (sie-KOH-sis) *(n)*: a severe mental disorder

pummel (PUH-muhl) *(v)*: to pound or beat, usually used in reference to fists

Q

quizzical (KWIH-zi-kuhl) *(adj)*: questioning; puzzled

R

radiance (RAY-dee-ants) *(n)*: the state or quality of being radiant, or bright

radiocarbon dating (ray-dee-oh-KAHR-buhn DAYT-ing) *(n)*: a method of determining the approximate age of an object by measuring the amount of radioactive carbon it contains

redeem (ri-DEEM) *(v)*: to take action to make up for wrongdoing; make amends for past deeds; to turn in for something of value

regime (ruh-ZHEEM) *(n)*: a government in power

regrettable (ri-GREH-tuh-buhl) *(adj)*: deserving regret; unfortunate

remorse (ri-MAWRS) *(n)*: regret for wrongdoing

repetitive (ri-PEH-ti-tiv) *(adj)*: tending to repeat

reproduce (ree-pruh-DOOS) *(v)*: to make a copy of; to produce (new individuals of the same kind) by sexual or asexual means

resourceful (ri-SAWRS-fuhl) *(adj)*: able to handle challenges creatively and effectively

resources (REE-sawr-sez) *(n)*: supplies that can meet a need; materials available for use

retract (ri-TRAKT) *(v)*: to draw back; take back

rhetorical question (ri-TAWR-i-kuhl KWES-chuhn) *(n)*: a question asked only for effect, not to get an answer

rhinestone (RINE-stone) *(n)*: a bright, colorless artificial gem often made of glass

ruthless (ROOTH-lis) *(adj)*: unfeeling; cruel; merciless

S

salutary (SAL-yuh-ter-ee) *(adj)*: having a healthy or beneficial effect

scornfully (SKAWRN-fuh-lee) *(adv)*: with feelings of hatred or disrespect

security (si-KYOOR-i-tee) *(n)*: freedom from danger; safety

semiconscious (seh-me-KON-shuhs) *(adj)*: not fully conscious

semiskilled (seh-mee-SKILD) *(adj)*: having limited skills or training

silhouette (sih-lih-WET) *(n)*: an outline of a figure; also, a profile portrait

silo (SIE-loh) *(n)*: a pit or cylindrical building in which food for livestock is stored

singular (SING-gyuh-ler) *(adj)*: exceptional; remarkable

sinister (SI-nuhs-ter) *(adj)*: wicked; evil

slander (SLAN-der) *(n)*: an oral statement that is untrue and hurts a person's reputation

sloop (sloop) *(n)*: a sailboat with a single mast

smirk (smurk) *(v)*: to smile in an annoyingly self-satisfied way

soundly (SOUND-lee) *(adv)*: without trouble or interruption; with sensibility and good judgment

sparse (spahrs) *(adj)*: few and scattered; thinly spread

spyware (SPAHY-wair) *(n)*: software that enables someone to obtain information about a person's computer activities without that person's knowledge

statesmanship (STAYTS-muhn-ship) *(n)*: the qualities, abilities, or methods of a statesman; skill in handling public affairs

steadfast (STED-fast) *(adj)*: firm in belief; unwavering; loyal

stereotype (STER-ee-uh-type) *(n)*: an over-simplified, often unfair, notion or way of thinking, as of a person or group, held by a number of people

strategically (struh-TEE-jih-klee) *(adv)*: as part of a plan

substantial (suhb-STAN-shuhl) *(adj)*: of a considerable or significant amount, quantity, or size

superficial (soo-per-FIH-shuhl) *(adj)*: limited to the surface; shallow

supernatural (soo-per-NAH-chuh-ruhl) *(adj)*: beyond what is usual or normal; that cannot be explained by the laws of nature

supervision (soo-per-VIH-zhuhn) *(n)*: overseeing; direction

survival (ser-VIE-vuhl) *(n)*: staying alive; outlasting others

synchronize (SING-kruh-nize) *(v)*: to cause to agree in time

T

tantalize (TAN-teh-lize) *(v)*: to tempt or torment, as by offering something desirable but withholding it

temperate zone (TEM-per-it zone) *(n)*: the area of Earth's surface between the tropics and the polar circles

tension (TEN-shuhn) *(n)*: tense state or condition; stress; anxiety

testimony (TES-tuh-moh-nee) *(n)*: oral statements sworn to be true in a court of law

titanic (tie-TA-nik) *(adj)*: having great size or power; colossal; immense

tragedy (TRA-juh-dee) *(n)*: a disastrous or very sad event

transfusion (trans-FYOO-zhuhn) *(n)*: transferring blood from one person to another

transmit (trans-MIT) *(v)*: to pass on; convey

tropical rain forest (TRAH-pi-kuhl rain FAWR-ist) *(n)*: a dense tropical woodland having a yearly rainfall of 100 inches or more and characterized by tall, broad-leaved evergreen trees and lush vegetation

U

upheaval (up-HEE-vuhl) *(n)*: severe or sudden disturbance or disorder

uproar (UP-rawr) *(n)*: a state of commotion or noisy disturbance

V

veranda (vuh-RAN-duh) *(n)*: an open porch, usually roofed, along one or more sides of a building

verdict (VUR-dikt) *(n)*: the decision of a judge or jury

verify (VER-uh-fie) *(v)*: to establish the accuracy or truth of; confirm

vice versa (VIE-suh VUR-suh) *(adv)*: the order or relation reversed; the other way around

W

wayward (WAY-werd) *(adj)*: going one's own way; unruly; willful

webinar (WEB-ih-nahr) *(n)*: a live educational seminar or presentation on the Internet, during which participants can usually ask questions

wily (WYE-lee) *(adj)*: crafty; sly

Index